CONFORMITY

CONFORMITY

The Power of Social Influences

Cass R. Sunstein

NEW YORK UNIVERSITY PRESS

New York

NEW YORK UNIVERSITY PRESS
New York
www.nyupress.org

References to Internet websites (URLs) were accurate at the time of writing.
Neither the author nor New York University Press is responsible for URLs
that may have expired or changed since the manuscript was prepared.

Library of Congress Cataloging-in-Publication Data
Names: Sunstein, Cass R., author.
Title: Conformity : the power of social influences / Cass R. Sunstein.
Description: New York : New York University Press, 2019. |
Also available as an ebook. | Includes bibliographical references and index.
Identifiers: LCCN 2018041768| ISBN 9781479867837 (cl ; alk. paper)
Subjects: LCSH: Sociological jurisprudence. | Law—Social aspects. |
Conformity. | Social influence.
Classification: LCC K370 .S83 2019 | DDC 340/.115—dc23
LC record available at https://lccn.loc.gov/2018041768

New York University Press books are printed on acid-free paper, and
their binding materials are chosen for strength and durability.
We strive to use environmentally responsible suppliers and materials
to the greatest extent possible in publishing our books.

Manufactured in the United States of America

10 9 8 7 6 5 4 3 2 1

Also available as an ebook

CONTENTS

ACKNOWLEDGMENTS

This short book has traveled a long and winding road. In early 2003, I delivered the Oliver Wendell Holmes, Jr., Lectures at Harvard Law School, under the title "Conformity and Dissent." With the help of the comments I received during and after the presentation, the lectures were reoriented, expanded, and transformed into a book, *Why Societies Need Dissent*, published by Harvard University Press in late 2003. There is of course a significant overlap between the original text and that book. But I retained a fondness for the original lecture text, which was not only significantly shorter but also more focused, less polemical, and a bit less preachy—and also more quizzical, and in some ways (I like to think) more enduring.

As of this writing, there is mounting worldwide attention to the problem of conformity, and also to associated questions about identity, extremism, cascades, polarization, and diversity. This book is a contemporary version of the original text, with a new preface and a variety of changes, mostly for updating and clarity of exposition. I am acutely aware that with respect to the underlying social science, there have been significant developments since 2003. I have done my best to summarize the leading developments and to avoid relying on controversial claims and findings, though the field continues to progress.

It took a village. For valuable discussions and comments, I am grateful to Jacob Gersen, Reid Hastie, David Hirshleifer, Christine Jolls, Catharine MacKinnon, Martha Nussbaum, Susan Moller Okin, Eric Posner, Richard Posner, Lior Strahilevitz, Edna Ullmann-Margalit, and Richard Zeckhauser. Special thanks to my agent, Sarah Chalfant, for help and support, and to my editor, Clara Platter, for valuable suggestions throughout and above all in connection with the preface. Andrew Heinrich and Cody Westphal provided excellent research assistance.

PREFACE

Conformity is as old as humanity. In the Garden of Eden, Adam followed Eve's lead. The spread of the world's great religions is partly a product of conformity. Books remain to be written on this topic, with special attention to Christianity, Islam, and Judaism.[1] Generosity and kindness, concern for the vulnerable, considerateness, protection of private property, respect for human dignity—all of these are fueled by conformity, which provides a kind of social glue.[2]

Conformity also makes atrocities possible. The Holocaust was many things, but it was emphatically a tribute to the immense power of conformity. The rise of Communism also reflected that power. Contemporary terrorism is not a product of poverty, mental illness, or a lack of education. It is a product, in large part, of the pressure that some people put on other people. That pressure has everything to do with conformity. When people of one political party march together, develop dogmas and rages, and ridicule people of another political party, conformity is at work. In its worst forms as well as its best, nationalism is fueled by conformity.

As we shall see, the idea of conformity is far more interesting and less simple than it seems. But two ideas capture much of the territory. First, the actions and statements of other people provide *information about what is true and what is right.* If your friends and neighbors worship a particular God, fear immigration, love a nation's current leader, believe that climate change is a hoax, or think that genetically modified food is dangerous to eat, you have reason to believe all those things. You might well take their beliefs as evidence of what you should believe.

Second, the actions and statements of other people tell you what you ought to do and say *if you want to remain in their good graces* (or get there in the first place). Even if you disagree with them in your heart of hearts, you might silence yourself or even agree with them in their presence. Once you do that, you might find yourself starting to shift internally. You might begin to act and even to think as they do.

The subject of conformity is not limited to any particular time and place, and I hope that the same is true of the discussion of that subject here. But it is worth noting that modern technologies—and above all the Internet—cast long-standing phenomena in a new light. Suppose that you live in a small, remote village, with a high degree of homogeneity. What you know will be mostly limited to what is known in that village. Your beliefs might well mirror those of your neighbors. You might be entirely rational, but what you believe might not be rational at all. As Justice Louis Brandeis noted, "Men feared witches and burnt women."[3]

Unless your own imagination and experiences lead you in fresh directions, you will act and think as your neighbors do. To be sure, some people are rebels, and they can add to a society's stock of information. For them, deviance is far more appealing than conformity. They *want* to be deviants. But if your world is limited, your horizons will be limited as well. There will be limits to what you can see and imagine.

Now suppose that wherever you live, you spend much of your time online. In some ways, the entire world is at your disposal. If you do a search for "the world's religions," you can learn a great deal in an extraordinarily short time. If you do a search for "climate change hoax," you can discover diverse views, and if you are willing to spend an hour or two on the topic, you can obtain at least a rough understanding of what scientists think. If you search for "genetically modified food health risks," you can find studies of multiple kinds and various reports, some of them highly technical. Sorting out what is reliable may not be easy. There are countless falsehoods out there. But here is the point: if you are inclined to conform, you will have to do a fair bit of work before you decide what, or whom, you will conform *to*.

In most ways, that is an immense step forward for the human species. Our potential horizons are far broader than they ever were, and they are getting broader all the time. At the same time, human beings appear to be *tribal*. Wherever we live—a small village or New York, Copenhagen, Jerusalem, Paris, Rome, Beijing, or Moscow—we develop allegiances. Once we do that, we follow informational signals from some people rather than others. We want the approval of those we love, admire, like, and trust. For that reason, conformity pressures will remain, even if there are a lot of tribes out there and even if we have some freedom to choose among them. (I once asked a new friend why we liked each other so much. Her answer came back immediately: "Same tribe.")

As I write, the world seems to be witnessing a rebirth of tribalism. In the United States, Europe, and South America, people seem to be sorting themselves into identifiable tribes, defined in terms of politics, religion, race, and ethnicity. Appearances can be misleading, of course, and to know whether there really is any such rebirth, we would need some careful analysis. But there is no question that for numerous people, the Internet in general and social media in particular are giving rise to new opportunities for conformity pressures.

Begin with informational signals: On your Facebook page or your Twitter feed, you might receive all sorts of material from people that you like or trust. They might tell you something about a nation's leader, crime, Russia, the Federal Bureau of Investigation, the European Union, a new product, how to raise children, or a new political movement—anything at all. What they say might be credible because they say it. Turn now to your concern for your reputation and social standing: If those in your online community think a certain way, you might be disinclined to disagree with them or inclined to agree with them. Of course much will depend on the thinness or the thickness of your connections with them. Perhaps you don't much care about what they think of you. But many people do care—which means they will be inclined to conform.

No simple evaluation of conformity would make the slightest sense. On the one hand, it helps to make civilization possible. On the other hand, it enables horrors and destroys creativity. My emphasis here is on the dynamics of conformity—on what it does and how it does it. The overall evaluation is, I hope, appreciative of nuance. If the discussion turns out to be most spirited when invoking misfits and rebels, well, I couldn't help myself.

For all the good that conformity does, it can also crush what is most precious and most vital in the human soul. Bob Dylan put it mysteriously and I think well: "To live outside the law, you must be honest."[4]

Introduction

The Power of Social Influences

How do people influence each other? What are the social functions of dissenters, malcontents, misfits, and skeptics? How do the answers to these questions bear on social stability, on the emergence of social movements, on law and policy, and on the design of private and public institutions? For orientation, consider three sets of clues.

1. A few years ago, a number of citizens from two different cities were assembled into small groups, usually consisting of six people.[1] The groups were asked to deliberate on three of the most contested issues of the time: climate change, affirmative action, and same-sex unions. The two cities were Boulder, known by its voting patterns to be predominantly left of center, and Colorado Springs, known by its voting patterns to be predominantly conservative. Citizens were first asked to record their views individually and anonymously, and then to deliberate together in an effort to reach a group decision. After deliberation, individual participants were asked to record their postdeliberation views individually and anonymously. What do you think happened?

As a result of group deliberation, people from Boulder moved to the left on all three issues. By contrast, people from

Colorado Springs became a lot more conservative. The effect of group deliberation was to shift individual opinions toward extremism. Group "verdicts" on climate change, affirmative action, and same-sex unions were more extreme than the predeliberation average of group members. In addition, the *anonymous* views of individual members became more extreme, after deliberation, than were their anonymous views before they started to talk.

As a result, deliberation sharply increased the disparities between the citizens of Boulder and those of Colorado Springs. Before deliberation, there was considerable overlap between many individuals in the two cities. After deliberation, the overlap was a lot smaller. Liberals and conservatives became more sharply divided. They started to live in different political universes.

2. Ordinary citizens were asked to say, as individuals, how much a wrongdoer should be punished for specified misconduct.[2] Their responses were measured on a scale of 0 to 8, where 0 meant no punishment at all and 8 meant "extremely severe" punishment. After offering their individual judgments, people were sorted into six-person juries, which were asked to deliberate and to reach unanimous verdicts. When the individual jurors favored little punishment, deliberating juries showed a "leniency shift," meaning a rating that was systematically *lower* than the median rating of individual members before they started to talk with one another. In other words, juries ended up more lenient than their own median juror in advance of deliberation.

But when individual jurors favored strong punishment, the group as a whole produced a "severity shift," meaning a rating that was systematically *higher* than the median rating of individual members before they started to talk. Thus, deliberating juries turned out to be more severe than their own median juror. The direction and the extent of the shift were determined by the median rating of individual jurors. When individuals started out with lenient ratings, groups became more lenient still. When individuals started out with severe ratings, groups became more severe still. It is worth emphasizing the latter finding: if group members are outraged, groups end up becoming even more outraged.

3. In the United States, a large number of judicial votes and decisions were investigated to see if judges on federal courts of appeals are influenced by other judges with whom they are sitting on three-judge panels.[3] It is tempting to speculate that judges will vote in accordance with their views about the law and will not be influenced by conformity pressures. But this suggestion turns out to be wrong.

A Republican-appointed judge sitting with two other judges appointed by Republican presidents becomes much more likely to vote in a stereotypically conservative direction in cases that involve civil rights, sexual harassment, environmental protection, and much more. Perhaps more remarkably, a Democratic-appointed judge sitting with two Republican appointees also becomes more likely to vote in a stereotypically conservative direction. And something important happens when three Republican appointees sit together: the likelihood of a stereotypically conservative result skyrockets. Democratic appointees show a similar pattern. When three such appointees sit together, a stereotypically liberal leaning is highly likely.

In short, how Democratic appointees and Republican appointees vote is very much dependent on whether they are sitting with one or two judges appointed by presidents of the same party. There is an unmistakable pattern of conformity: when sitting with Republican appointees, Democratic appointees often vote like Republican appointees, and when sitting with Democratic appointees, Republican-appointed judges often vote like Democratic appointees.

For each of us, conformity is often a rational course of action, but when all or most of us conform, society can end up making large mistakes. One reason we conform is that we often lack much information of our own—about health, about investments, about law, and about politics—and the decisions of others provide the best available information about what should be done. The central problem is that widespread conformity deprives the public of information that it needs to have. Conformists are often thought to be protective of social interests, keeping quiet for the sake of the group, while dissenters tend to be seen as selfish individualists, embarking on projects of their own. But in an important sense, the opposite is closer to the truth. In many situations, dissenters benefit others, while conformists benefit themselves.

In a well-functioning democracy, institutions reduce the risks that accompany conformity, in part because they ensure that conformists will see and learn from dissenters, and hence increase the likelihood that more information will emerge, to the benefit of all. A high-level official during World War II attributed the successes of the Allies, and the failures of Hitler and the other Axis powers, to the greater ability of citizens in democracies to scrutinize and dissent, and hence to improve past and proposed courses of action, including those that involve military operations.[4] Scrutiny and dissent were possible because skeptics were not punished by the law and because informal punishments, in the form of social pressures, were relatively weak.

With this claim in mind, I will suggest that an understanding of group influences and their potentially harmful effects casts new light on a wide range of issues, including the nature of well-functioning constitutional structures; extremism; the rise of authoritarianism; the importance of the separation of powers; the problem of "echo chambers"; the prerequisites of a system of freedom of speech; the defining characteristics of liberal political orders; the vices and virtues of contemporary social media; the functions of bicameralism; the constraining effects of social norms; the sources of ethnic hostility and political radicalism; the importance of civil liberties in wartime and during social panics and witch hunts; the performance of juries; the effects of diversity on the federal judiciary; affirmative action in higher education; and the potentially large consequences of law even when it is never enforced.

Throughout I focus on two influences on individual belief and behavior. The first involves the information conveyed by the actions and statements of other people. If a number of people seem to believe that some proposition is true, there is reason to believe that that proposition is in fact true. Most of what we think—about facts, morality, and law—is a product not of firsthand knowledge but of what we learn from what others do and think. This is true even though they too may be merely following the crowd. In life, that can be a massive problem. In law, this phenomenon can create serious problems for the system of precedent, as when courts of appeals follow previous courts that are in turn following their predecessors, creating a danger of widespread, self-perpetuating error. We can see these problems as important in themselves and also as a metaphor for many social phenomena.

It is also true that some people have far more influence than others, simply because the decisions of those people convey more information. We are especially likely to follow those who are confident ("the confidence heuristic"), who have special expertise, who seem most like us, who fare best, or whom we otherwise have reason to trust. It is worth underlining the phrase "most like us"; for better or for worse, those are the people whose beliefs often have the largest impact on our own.

The second influence is the pervasive human desire to have and to retain the good opinion of others. If a number of people seem to believe something, there is reason not to disagree with them, at least not in public. The desire to maintain the good opinion of others breeds conformity and squelches dissent, especially but not only in groups that are connected by bonds of loyalty and affection, which can therefore prevent learning, entrench falsehoods, increase dogmatism, and impair group performance. In the highest reaches of government—including the White House—this can be a serious problem. We shall see that close-knit groups, discouraging conflict and disagreement, often do badly for that very reason. In any case much of human behavior is a product of social influences. For example, employees are far more likely to file suit if members of the same work group have also done so;[5] teenage girls who see that other teenagers are having children are more likely to become pregnant themselves;[6] the perceived behavior of others has a large effect on the level of violent crime;[7] broadcasters mimic one another, producing otherwise inexplicable fads in programming;[8] and lower courts sometimes do the same, especially in highly technical areas, and hence judicial mistakes may never be corrected.[9]

We should not lament social influences or wish them away. Much of the time, people do better when they take close account of what others do. Some of the time, we even do best to follow others blindly. But social influences also diminish the total level of information within any group, and they threaten, much of the time, to lead individuals and institutions in the wrong directions. Dissent can be an important corrective; many groups and institutions have too little of it.[10]

As we shall see, conformists are free riders, whereas dissenters often confer benefits on others. It is tempting to free ride. As we shall also see, social pressures are likely to lead groups of like-minded people to extreme positions. When groups become caught up in hatred and violence, it is rarely because of economic deprivation[11] or primordial suspicions;[12] it is far more often a product of the informational and reputational influences discussed here.[13] Indeed, unjustified extremism frequently results from a "crippled epistemology," in which extremists react to a small subset of relevant information, coming mostly from one another.[14]

Similar processes occur in less dramatic forms. Many large-scale shifts within legislatures, bureaucracies, and courts are best explained by reference to social influences. When a legislature suddenly shows concern with some formerly neglected problem—for example, unlawful immigration, climate change, hazardous waste dumps, or corporate misconduct—the concern is often a product of conformity effects, not of real engagement with the problem. Of course the new concern might be justified. But if social influences are encouraging people to conceal information that they have, or if the blind are leading the blind, serious problems are likely.

There is a further point. With relatively small "shocks," similar groups can be led, by social pressures, to dramatically different beliefs and actions. When societies differ, or when large-scale changes occur over time, the reason often lies not where we usually look but in small and sometimes elusive factors.[15] Serendipity is often the best explanation for major shifts; deep explanations about culture or the march of history are comforting but wrong.

An appreciation of informational influences and of people's concern for the good opinion of others helps to show how, and when, law can alter behavior without being enforced—and merely by virtue of the signal that it provides. The central point here is that law can provide reliable evidence both about what should be done and about what most people think should be done. In either case, it can convey a great deal of relevant information. Consider bans on public smoking and on sexual harassment. If people think the law is speaking for the view of most or all, potential violators are less likely to smoke or to engage in sexual harassment. Potential victims are also more likely to take the steps to enforce the law privately, as, for example, through reminding people of their legal responsibilities and insisting that violators come into compliance. The #MeToo movement of 2017 and 2018 had many causes, and it is closely connected with several of the phenomena on which I will focus here; the law, forbidding sexual harassment, helped make it possible.

In this light we can better understand the much-disputed claim that the law has an "expressive function."[16] By virtue of that function, law can even stop or accelerate a social cascade. Here too the areas of cigarette smoking and sexual harassment are relevant examples. And the #MeToo movement can be seen as a cascade. But if would-be violators are part of a dissident subcommunity, they might well be able to resist law's expressive effect; fellow dissidents can band together and encourage one another to violate the law. Indeed, informational and reputational factors can even encourage widespread noncompliance, as, for example, in drug use and failure to comply with the tax laws.[17] The law's expressive power is partly a function of its moral authority, and when law lacks that authority within a subcommunity, its signal may be irrelevant or even counterproductive. The law may say "no!" but some people will want to say "yes!"

This book is divided into four chapters. In chapter 1, I develop a central unifying theme, which is that in many contexts, individuals are suppressing their private signals—about what is true and what is right—and that this suppression can cause significant social harm. In chapter 2, I turn to social cascades, by which an idea or a practice spreads rapidly from one person to another, potentially leading to radical shifts. Focusing on group polarization, chapter 3 investigates how, why, and when groups of like-minded people go to extremes.

Chapter 4 explores institutions. I urge that the principal contribution of the framers of the U.S. Constitution lay both in their endorsement of deliberative democracy and in their insistence that cognitive diversity is an affirmative good, likely to improve deliberation. This enthusiasm for cognitive diversity helps account for the systems of checks and balances and federalism. I also suggest that it is important to attempt to provide a mix of views on the federal bench; indeed, consideration should be given to increasing the likelihood that panels, on courts of appeals, contain judges appointed by the president of different parties.

The analysis of diversity on the federal judiciary is of interest in itself, but I intend it also as an example of a large number of contexts in which cognitive diversity is important and in which conformity can have baleful effects. I urge as well that in those cases in which racial diversity will improve discussion, it is entirely legitimate for colleges and universities to attempt to promote racial diversity.

CHAPTER 1

How Conformity Works

Why, and when, do people do what others do? To answer this question, we need to distinguish between hard questions and easy ones. It is reasonable to speculate that when people are confident that they are right, they will be more willing to do what they think best and to reject the views of the crowd. Several sets of experiments confirm this speculation, but they also offer some significant twists. Most important, they suggest three points that I will emphasize throughout:

1. Those who are confident and firm will have particular influence, and can lead otherwise identical groups in dramatically different directions.
2. People are extremely vulnerable to the unanimous views of others, and hence a single dissenter, or voice of sanity, is likely to have a huge impact.
3. If people seem to be from some group we distrust or dislike, or a kind of "out group," they are far less likely to influence us, even on the simplest questions.[1] Indeed, we might say or do the very opposite ("reactive devaluation"). And if people are part of a group to which we also belong, they are far more likely to influence us, on both easy and hard questions. Bonds of affection have a large impact on how we react to what others say and do.

I shall have a fair bit to say about ordinary life, but my ultimate goal is to see how these points bear on policy and law. Let us begin by reviewing some classic studies.

Hard Questions

In the 1930s, the psychologist Muzafer Sherif conducted some simple experiments on sensory perception.[2] Subjects were placed in a very dark room, and a small pinpoint of light was positioned at some distance in front of them. Because of a perceptual illusion, the light, which was actually stationary, appeared to move. On each of several trials, Sherif asked people to estimate the distance that the light had moved. When polled individually, subjects did not agree with one another, and their answers varied from one trial to another. This is not surprising; because the light did not move, any judgment about distance was a stab in the dark.

But Sherif found some striking results when subjects were asked to act in small groups. Here the individual judgments converged, and a group norm, establishing the right distance, quickly developed. Indeed, the norm remained stable within groups across different trials, thus leading to a situation in which different groups made, and were committed to, quite different judgments.[3] There is an important clue here about how similar groups, indeed similar nations, can converge on very different beliefs and actions simply because of modest and even arbitrary variations in starting points. You can think of social media, and in some respects the Internet as a whole, as a contemporary version of Sherif's experiments.

People converge on group norms even if their individual judgments start in radically different places, and those norms become fairly stable over time. Different groups can end up in different epistemic universes, whether the issue involves immigration, sexual harassment, the Middle East, trade, or civil rights.

When Sherif added a confederate—his own ally, unbeknownst to subjects—something else happened.[4] The judgment of a single confederate, typically much higher or much lower than those made by individual subjects, had a major effect. It helped produce correspondingly higher or lower judgments within the group. The large lesson is that at least in cases involving difficult questions of fact, judgments "could be imposed by an individual who had no coercive power and no special claim to expertise, only a willingness to be consistent and unwavering in the face of others' uncertainty."[5]

Perhaps more remarkable still, the group's judgments became thoroughly *internalized*, so that subjects would adhere to them even when reporting on their own, even a year later, and even when participating in new groups whose members offered different judgments. The initial judgments were also found to have effects across "generations." In an experiment in which fresh subjects were introduced and others retired, so that eventually all participants were new to the situation, the original group judgment tended to stick, even after the person who was originally responsible for it had been long gone.[6] In this small experiment, there are two lessons about the formation and longevity of some cultural beliefs and practices: a single person, or a small group, may be responsible for them, and over a long period, these beliefs and practices can be enduring and become defining.

What accounts for these results? The most obvious answer points to the informational influences produced by other people's judgments. After all, the apparent movements are a perceptual illusion, and the system of perception does not readily assign distances to those movements. In those circumstances, people are especially likely to be swayed by a confident and consistent group member. If one person seems clear about the distance, why not believe that person? There is considerable theoretical and empirical work on "the confidence heuristic," which means that people are more likely to follow those who express their views confidently, assuming that confidently expressed views signal better information.[7] Sherif's finding has implications outside of the laboratory and for classrooms, workplaces, courtrooms, bureaucracies, and legislatures. If uninformed people are trying to decide whether immigration or climate change is a serious problem, or whether they should be concerned about existing levels of arsenic in drinking water, they are likely to be responsive to the views of confident and consistent others.[8]

What is true for factual issues is true for moral, political, and legal issues as well. Suppose that a group of legislators is trying to decide how to handle a highly technical issue. If a "confederate" is planted among the group, showing considerable confidence, that person is highly likely to be able to move the group in that individual's preferred direction. So too if the person is not a confederate at all but simply a friend, neighbor, colleague, boss, or legislator with great confidence on the issue at hand. If public officials or judges are trying to resolve a complex issue on which they lack certainty, they too are vulnerable to conformity effects. And for judicial panels as well, Sherif-type effects can be expected on technical matters if one judge is confident and seems expert. The problem is that the so-called specialists may have biases and agendas of their own, leading to large errors. But there is an important qualification to these claims, to which I will return: Sherif's conformity findings significantly decrease if the experimenter uses a confederate whose membership in a different social group is made salient to subjects.[9] If you know that the confident person belongs to a group different from yours—one that you distrust or dislike—you might not be influenced at all.

Easy Questions

But what if perception does provide reliable guidance? What if people have good reason to know the right answer? Some famous experiments, conducted by Solomon Asch, explored whether people would be willing to overlook the apparently unambiguous evidence of their own senses.[10] In those experiments, the subject was placed into a group of seven to nine people who seemed to be other subjects in the experiment but who were actually Asch's confederates. The simple task was to "match" a particular line, shown on a large white card, to one of the three "comparison lines" that was identical to it in length. The two nonmatching lines were substantially different, with the differential varying from an inch and three quarters to three quarters of an inch.

In the first two rounds of the Asch experiments, everyone agrees about the right answer. "The discriminations are simple; each individual monotonously calls out the same judgment."[11] But "suddenly this harmony is disturbed at the third round."[12] All other group members make what is obviously, to the subject and to any reasonable person, a clear error, matching the line at issue to one that is conspicuously longer or shorter. In these circumstances, the subject, in almost all cases showing initial confusion and disbelief at the apparent mistakes of others, has a choice: he can maintain independent judgment or instead accept the view of the unanimous majority. What would you do? As it turns out, a large number of people end up yielding at least once in a series of trials. They defy the evidence of their own senses and agree with everyone else.

When asked to decide on their own, subjects erred less than 1 percent of the time. But in rounds in which group pressure supported the wrong answer, subjects erred no less than 36.8 percent of the time.[13] Indeed, in a series of twelve questions, no less than 70 percent of subjects went along with the group and defied the evidence of their own senses, at least once.[14] We should not overstate this finding. Most people, most of the time, say what they actually see. But Asch's most noteworthy finding is that most people, some of the time, are willing to yield, even in the face of clear reason indicating that the group is wrong.

Conformity experiments of this kind have produced more than 130 sets of results from seventeen countries, including Zaire, Germany, France, Japan, Lebanon, and Kuwait.[15] A meta-analysis of these studies uncovered a variety of refinements of Asch's basic findings, with significant cultural differences, but it is fair to say that his basic conclusions hold up. For all results, the mean percentage error is 29 percent.[16] People in some nations, with "conformist" cultures, do err more than people in other nations, with more "individualist" cultures.[17] The variations are real, but the overall pattern of errors—with subjects conforming between 20 and 40 percent of the time— shows the power of conformity across many nations.

Note that Asch's findings contain two conflicting lessons. First, a significant number of people are independent all or much of the time. About 25 percent of people are consistently independent;[18] such people are uninfluenced by the group. Moreover, about two-thirds of total individual answers do not conform. Hence "there is evidence of extreme individual differences" in susceptibility to group influences, with some people remaining completely independent and others "going with the majority without exception."[19] While independent subjects "present a striking spectacle to an observer," giving "the appearance of being unshakable,"[20] other people show a great deal of anxiety and confusion.[21] Second, most subjects, at least some of the time, are willing to yield to the group *even on an apparently easy question on which they have direct and unambiguous evidence.*

For present purposes, the latter finding is the most relevant. It suggests that even when we see something very clearly, many or most of us might say, "If everyone else sees otherwise, we should go along with them." There is a large lesson here about why people might seem to agree with stupid or horrible things—about science, about politics, and about members of different religious, ethnic, and racial groups. There is a lesson too about why different groups can go in radically different directions, even with respect to questions of fact. They might be interacting with the equivalent of Asch's confederates.

Reasons and Blunders

Why do people sometimes ignore the evidence of their own senses? The two principal explanations involve information and peer pressure. Some of Asch's subjects seem to have thought that the unanimous confederates must be right. But other people, though believing that group members were unaccountably mistaken, were unwilling to make, in public, what those members would see as an error. They falsified their own views. They said something they believed to be untrue.

In Asch's own studies, several conformists said, in private interviews, that their own opinions must have been wrong[22]—suggesting that information, rather than peer pressure, is what was moving them.[23] This informational account is strengthened by a study in which people recorded their answers anonymously but gave nearly as many wrong answers as they had under Asch's own conditions.[24] A similar study finds that conformity is not much lower when the subject's response is unavailable to the majority.[25]

On the other hand, these are unusual results, and experimenters generally do find significantly reduced error, in the same basic circumstances as Asch's experiments, when subjects are asked to give a purely private answer.[26] This finding suggests that people did not really believe their own senses were misleading them; they were trying instead not to look stupid in front of other people. And in experiments in which conformity or deviation is made very visible, conformity grows.[27] The finding also suggests that peer pressure matters a great deal and helps explain Asch's findings.

Asch's own conclusion was that his results raised the possibility that "the social process is polluted" by the "dominance of conformity."[28] He added, "That we have found the tendency to conformity in our society so strong that reasonably intelligent and well-meaning young people are willing to call white black is a matter of concern."[29] As I have noted, Asch's experiments produce broadly similar findings across nations, and so in Asch's sentence just quoted, the word "society" could well be replaced with the word "world."

We should stress a separate point here: many people are not willing to disclose their own information to the group, even though it is in the group's interest to learn what is known or thought by individual members. To see this point, imagine a group almost all of whose members believe something to be true even though it is false. Imagine too that one member of the group or a very few members of the group know the truth. Are they likely to correct the dominant view? If Asch's findings generalize, the answer is that they may not be. They are not reticent because they are irrational. They are making a perfectly sensible response to the simple fact that the dominant view is otherwise—a fact that suggests either that the small minority is wrong or that they are likely to risk their own reputations if they insist they are right. As we shall see, Asch's findings help explain why groups can end up making unfortunate and even self-destructive decisions.

There have been significant developments, of course, in the decades since Asch did his original research. Some of the most interesting work makes a sharp distinction between compliance and acceptance.[30] People *comply* when they defer to others whom they believe to be wrong. In that case, they will conform in public but not in private. People *accept* when they internalize the view of the group. As we have seen, Asch's findings involve a degree of both compliance and acceptance. More recent empirical work also finds evidence of both, with a further finding that as the size of the majority expands, compliance increases.[31]

Both theoretical and empirical research has also explored whether conformity works by changing people's beliefs or instead their preferences and tastes, finding that researchers have focused excessively on the former.[32] There has been important clarifying work about the kinds of activities that will see high levels of conformity, and thus fads and fashions.[33] We also know more about the kinds of people who are most likely to conform[34] and the circumstances that heighten or diminish conformity in Asch-like settings. If, for example, people are reminded of circumstances in which they have acted without inhibition, they are more likely to conform.[35] In general, and with qualifications that are not central to my argument here, Asch's central findings have held up.

Would those findings apply to judgments about morality, policy, and law? It seems jarring to think that people would yield to a unanimous group when the question involves a moral, political, or legal issue on which they have great confidence. But if Asch is correct, such yielding should be expected, at least some of the time. We will find powerful evidence that this happens within federal courts of appeals in the United States. The deadening effect of public opinion was of course a central concern of John Stuart Mill, who insisted that protection "against the tyranny of the magistrate is not enough" and that it was also important to protect "against the tyranny of the prevailing opinion and feeling; against the tendency of society to impose, by other means than civil penalties, its own ideas and practices as rules of conduct on those who dissent from them."[36]

Mill's focus here is on the adverse effects of conformity not only on the individuals who are thus tyrannized but also on society itself, which is deprived of important information. I do not think it irrelevant that the love of Mill's life started as an illicit affair. (His lover and eventual wife, Harriet Taylor, was married when their relationship began.) Mill's relationship with Taylor produced widespread opprobrium in their circles and a rupture from his own family. In his writing, Mill celebrated freedom from social convention and "experiments of living." His attack on conformity was general, emphasizing as it did the importance of following one's own path, free of "the tyranny of the prevailing opinion and feeling." But Mill practiced what he preached. The idea of "experiments of living" deserves emphasis in the annals of freedom.

How to Increase (or Decrease) Conformity

What factors increase or decrease conformity? Consistent with Sherif's findings, people are less likely to conform if they have high social status or are extremely confident about their own views.[37] They are more likely to conform if the task is difficult or if they are frightened.[38] Consider some other ways to make conformity more or less likely.

Financial Rewards

Financial rewards for correct answers affect performance, and in two different ways.[39] When people stand to make money if they are right, the rate of conformity is significantly *decreased* in the same basic condition as the Asch experiments, so long as the task is easy. People are less willing to follow group members when they stand to profit from a correct answer. We can see why that happens. If you know what is right, and if you will make money by saying what is right, you will probably say what is right, even if people around you are blundering.

But there is a striking difference when the experiments are altered to make the underlying task difficult. In that event, a financial incentive, rewarding correct answers, actually *increases* conformity. People are more willing to follow the crowd when they stand to profit from a correct answer if the question is hard. Perhaps most strikingly, the level of conformity is about the same, when financial incentives are absent, in low-difficulty and high-difficulty tasks—but the introduction of financial rewards splits the results on those tasks dramatically apart, with significantly decreased conformity for low-difficulty tasks and significantly increased conformity for high-difficulty tasks.[40]

These results have straightforward explanations. A certain number of people, in the Asch experiments, actually know the right answer and give conforming answers only because it is not worthwhile to reject the shared view of others in public. But when a financial incentive is offered, peer pressure is outweighed by the possibility of material gain. The implication is that an economic reward can counteract the effects of social pressures. There is a lesson here for groups of all kinds—schools, private employers, and governments. If people know they will gain if they say what they know, then groups are more likely to obtain crucial information.

By contrast, difficult tasks leave people with a great deal of uncertainty about whether they are right. In such circumstances, people are all the more likely to give weight to the views of others, simply because those views may well be the most reliable source of information. If you are asked to solve a difficult math problem, or to describe the most sensible approach for reducing deaths on the highways, you might defer to the wisdom of the room. Consider in this regard the parallel finding that people's confidence in their own judgments is directly related to the confidence shown by the experimenter's confederates.[41] When the confederates act with confidence and enthusiasm, subjects also show heightened confidence in their judgments, even when they are simply following the crowd. Consider also the broad claim that imitation of most

other people can operate as a kind of "fast and frugal" heuristic, one that works well for many creatures, including human
beings, in a wide variety of settings.[42] If you are not sure what
to do, you might well do what others do. Like most heuristics,
the imitation heuristic, while generally sensible and often the
best available, produces errors in many situations.[43]

There is a disturbing implication. A "majority consensus"
is "often capable of misleading individuals into inaccurate,
irrational, or unjustified judgments." Such a consensus "can
also produce heightened confidence in such judgments as
well."[44] It follows that "so long as the judgments are difficult
or ambiguous, and the influencing agents are united and confident, increasing the importance of accuracy will heighten
confidence as well as conformity—a dangerous combination."[45] As we shall see, the point very much bears on the
sources of unjustified extremism, especially under circumstances in which countervailing information is unavailable.
Extremists are often following one another.

The Size of the Group

Asch's original studies found that varying the size of the
group of confederates, unanimously making the erroneous
decision, mattered only up to a number of three; increases
from that point had little effect.[46] Using one confederate did
not increase subjects' errors at all; using two confederates
increased errors to 13.6 percent; and using three confederates
increased errors to 31.8 percent, not substantially different from the level that emerged from further increases in

group size. But Asch's own findings appear unusual on this count. Subsequent studies have usually found that, contrary to Asch's own findings, increases in the size of the group of confederates do increase conformity.[47]

A Voice of Sanity

More significantly, a modest variation in the experimental conditions makes all the difference. The existence of at least one compatriot, or voice of sanity, dramatically reduces both conformity and error. When one confederate made a correct match, errors were reduced by three-quarters, even if there was a strong majority the other way.[48] There is a clear implication here: If a group is embarking on an unfortunate course of action, a single dissenter might be able to turn it around, by energizing ambivalent group members who would otherwise follow the crowd.

It follows that affective ties among members, making even a single dissent less likely, might well undermine the performance of groups and institutions. Consider here Brooke Harrington's brilliant study of the performance of investment clubs—small groups of people who pool their money to make joint decisions about stock market investments.[49] The worst-performing clubs were built on affective ties and primarily social; the best-performing clubs had limited social connections and were focused on increasing returns. Dissent was far more frequent in the high-performing clubs. The low performers usually had unanimous votes, with little open debate. Harrington found that the votes in low-performing groups were "cast to build social cohesion rather than to make the best financial choice."[50] In short, conformity resulted in significantly lower returns.

Being In or Out

Much depends on the subjects' perceived relationship to the experimenters' confederates and in particular on whether the subjects consider themselves to be part of the same group in which those confederates fall. If the subjects identify themselves as members of a different group from the majority, the conformity effect is greatly reduced.[51] People are especially likely to conform when the group consists of people whom subjects like or admire or with whom they otherwise feel connected.[52] The general point explains why group membership is often emphasized by those who seek to increase or decrease the influence of a certain point of view—such as conservatives, liberals, Catholics, Jews, socialists, Democrats, and Republicans. Perhaps advocates can be discredited, with the relevant group, by showing that they are "conservative" or "leftists," and so prone to offer unacceptable views. I have referred to the phenomenon of "reactive devaluation," by which people devalue arguments and positions simply because of their source.

Thus conformity—and potentially error—is dramatically increased, in public statements, when subjects perceive themselves as part of a reasonably discrete group that includes the experimenter's confederates (all of whom are psychology majors, for example).[53] By contrast, conformity is dramatically decreased, and error correspondingly decreased, in public statements when subjects perceive themselves as in a different group from the experimenter's confederates (all of whom are ancient history majors, for example).[54]

Notably, private opinions, expressed anonymously afterward, were about the same whether or not the subjects perceived themselves as members of the same group as others in the experiment. And people who thought they were members of the same group as the experimenter's confederates gave far more accurate answers, and far less conforming answers, when they were speaking privately.[55] In the real world, would-be dissenters might silence themselves when and because they are in a group of like-minded others—partly because they do not want to risk the opprobrium of those others and partly because they fear they will, through their dissent, weaken the effectiveness and reputation of the group to which they belong.

There is a large lesson here. Publicly expressed statements, showing agreement with a majority view, may be both wrong and insincere, especially when people think of themselves as members of the same group as the majority.[56] The finding of heightened conformity is linked with evidence of poor performance by groups whose members are connected by affective ties; in such groups, people are less likely to say what they know and more likely to suppress disagreement. A system of checks and balances, attempting to ensure that ambition will check ambition, can be understood as a way of increasing the likelihood of dissent and of decreasing the likelihood that members of any particular group, or institution, will be reluctant to disclose what they think and know.[57]

Shocks, Authority, and Expertise

In the Sherif and Asch experiments, no particular person has special expertise. No member of the group shows unusual measurement abilities or wonderful eyesight. But we might safely predict that subjects would be even more inclined to blunder if they had reason to believe that one or more of the experimenters' confederates was particularly likely to be correct. This hypothesis receives support from a possible interpretation of one of the most alarming findings in modern social science, involving conformity not to the judgments of peers but to the will of an experimenter.[58] These experiments are of independent interest, because they have implications for social influences on judgments of morality, not merely facts.

The experiments, conducted by the psychologist Stanley Milgram, ask people to administer electric shocks to a person sitting in an adjacent room.[59] Subjects are told, falsely, that the purpose of the experiment is to test the effects of punishment on memory. Unbeknownst to the subject, the victim of the electric shocks is a confederate and there are no real shocks. The apparent shocks are delivered by a simulated shock generator, offering thirty clearly delineated voltage levels, ranging from 15 to 450 volts, accompanied by verbal descriptions ranging from "slight shock" to "danger: severe shock."[60] As the experiment unfolds, the subject is asked to administer increasingly severe shocks for incorrect answers, up to and past the "danger: severe shock" level, which begins at 400 volts.

In Milgram's original experiments, the subjects included forty men between the ages of twenty and fifty. They came from a range of occupations, including engineers, high school teachers, and postal clerks.[61] They were paid $4.50 for their participation—and also told they could keep the money no matter how the experiment went. The "memory test" involved remembering word pairs; every mistake, by the confederate/victim, was to be met by an electric shock and a movement to one higher level on the shock generator. To ensure that everything seems authentic, the subject is, at the beginning of the experiment, given an actual sample shock at the lowest level. But the subject is also assured that the shocks are not dangerous, with the experimenter declaring, in response to a prearranged question from the confederate, "Although the shocks can be extremely painful, they cause no permanent tissue damage."[62]

In the original experiments, the victim does not make any protest until the 300-volt shock, which produces a loud kick, by the victim, on the wall of the room where he is bound to the electric chair. After that point, the victim does not answer further questions and is heard from only after the 315-volt shock, when he pounds on the wall again—and is not heard from thereafter, even with increases in shocks to and past the 400-volt level. If the subject indicates an unwillingness to continue, the experimenter offers prods of increasing firmness, from "Please go on" to "You have no other choice; you must go on."[63] But the experimenter has no power to impose sanctions on subjects.

Most people predict that in such studies, more than 95 percent of subjects would refuse to proceed to the end of the series of shocks. When people are asked to make predictions about what people would do, the expected breakoff point is "very strong shock,"[64] of 195 volts. But in Milgram's initial experiments, every one of the forty subjects went beyond 300 volts. The mean maximum shock level was 405 volts, and a strong majority—twenty-six out of forty, or 65 percent—went to the full 450-volt shock, two steps beyond "danger: severe shock."[65]

Later variations on the original experiments produced even more remarkable results. In those experiments, the victim expresses a growing level of pain and distress as the voltage increases.[66] Small grunts are heard from 75 volts to 105 volts, and at 120 volts, the subject shouts, to the experimenter, that the shocks are starting to become painful. At 150 volts, the victims cries out, "Experimenter, get me out of here! I won't be in the experiment any more! I refuse to go on!"[67] At 180 volts, the victim says, "I can't stand the pain." At 270 volts he responds with an agonized scream. At 300 volts he shouts that he will no longer answer the questions. At 315 volts he screams violently.

At 330 volts and after, he is not heard. In this version of the experiment, there is no significant change in Milgram's results: twenty-five of forty participants went to the maximum level, and the mean maximum level was over 360 volts. In a somewhat gruesome variation, the victim says, before the experiment begins, that he has a heart condition, and his pleas to discontinue the experiment include repeated reference to the fact his heart is "bothering" him as the shocks continue.[68] This too did not lead subjects to behave differently.[69] Notably, Milgram's basic findings were generally replicated in 2009, with only slightly lower obedience rates than

Milgram found forty-five years earlier; men and women did not differ in their rates of obedience.[70]

Milgram himself explains his results as showing obedience to authority, in a way reminiscent of the behavior of many Germans under Nazi rule, and indeed Milgram was partly motivated by the goal of understanding how the Holocaust could have happened.[71] Milgram concluded that ordinary people will follow orders even if the result is to produce great suffering in innocent others. Undoubtedly simple obedience is part of the picture. But there is another explanation.

Subjects who are invited to an academic setting, to participate in an experiment run by an apparently experienced scientist, might well defer to the experimenter's instructions in the belief that the experimenter is likely to know what should be done, all things considered. If the experimenter asks subjects to proceed, most subjects might believe, not unreasonably, that the harm apparently done to the victims is not serious and that the experiment actually has significant benefits for society. On this account, the experimenter has special expertise. And if Milgram's subjects believed something like this, they were actually correct!

If this account is right, then the participants in the Milgram experiments might be seen as similar to those in the Asch experiments, with the experimenter having a greatly amplified voice. Many of Asch's subjects were deferring to the informational signal given by unanimous others; Milgram's subjects were doing something similar. An expert or an authority can be a lot like unanimous others. And on this account, some or many of the subjects might have put their moral qualms to one side, not because of blind obedience but because of a judgment that those qualms are likely to have been ill founded. That judgment might be based in turn on a belief that the experimenter is not likely to ask subjects to proceed if the experiment is truly harmful or objectionable.

In short, Milgram's subjects might be responding to an especially loud informational signal—the sort of signal sent by a specialist or a crowd. And on this view, Milgram was wrong to draw an analogy between the behavior of his subjects and the behavior of Germans under Hitler. His subjects were not simply obeying a leader but responding to someone whose credentials and good faith they thought they could trust. Of course it is not simple, in theory or in practice, to distinguish between obeying a leader and accepting the beliefs of an expert. The only suggestion is that the obedience of subjects was hardly baseless; it involved a setting in which subjects had some reason to think that the experimenter was not asking them to produce serious physical harm out of sadism or for no reason at all.

I do not argue that this explanation provides a full account of Milgram's contested findings. But a subsequent study, exploring the grounds of obedience, offers support for this interpretation.[72] In that study, a large number of subjects watched the tapes of the Milgram experiments and were asked to rank possible explanations for compliance with the experimenter's request. Deference to expertise was the highest-ranked option. This is not definitive, of course, but an illuminating variation on the basic experiment, by Milgram himself, provides further support.[73] In this variation, the subject is among three people asked to administer the shocks, and two of those people, actually confederates, refuse to go past a certain level (150 volts for one and 210 volts for the other). In such cases, the overwhelming majority of subjects—92.5 percent—defy the experimenter.[74] This was by far the most effective of Milgram's many variations on his basic study, all designed to reduce the level of obedience.[75]

Why was the defiance of peers so potent? I suggest that the subjects, in this variation, were very much like those subjects who had at least one supportive confederate in Asch's experiments. One such confederate led Asch's subjects to say what they saw; so too, peers who acted on the basis of conscience freed Milgram's subjects to give less weight to the instructions of the experimenter and to follow their consciences as well. Milgram himself established, in yet another variation, that without any advice from the experimenter and without any external influences at all, the subject's moral judgment was clear: do not administer shocks above a very low level.[76]

Indeed, that moral judgment had nearly the same degree of clarity, to Milgram's subjects, as the clear and correct factual judgments made by Asch's subjects when they were deciding about the length of lines on their own (and hence not confronted with Asch's confederates). In Milgram's experiments, it was the experimenter's own position—that the shocks should continue and that no permanent damage would be done—that had a high degree of influence, akin to the influence of Asch's unanimous confederates. But when the subject's peers rejected the position of Milgram's experimenter, the informational content of that position was effectively negated by the information presented by the refusals of peers. Hence subjects could rely on their own moral judgments or even follow the moral signals indicated by the peers' refusals.

Then and now, the best interpretation of Milgram's findings is less than clear, but the general lessons are not obscure. When the morality of a situation is not evident, people are likely to be influenced by someone who seems to be an expert, able to weigh the concerns and risks involved. But when the expert's questionable moral judgment is countered by reasonable people who bring their own moral judgments to bear, people become less likely to follow experts. They are far more likely to do as their conscience dictates.

As we shall see, compliance with law has similar features. A legal pronouncement about what should be done will often operate in the same way as an expert judgment about what should be done. It follows that many people will follow the law even when it is hardly ever enforced—and even if they would otherwise be inclined to question the judgment that the law embodies. But if peers are willing to violate the law, violations may become widespread, especially but not only if people think that the law is enjoining them from doing something that they wish to do, either for selfish reasons or for reasons of principle. In this way, Milgram's experiments offer some lessons about when law will be ineffective unless vigorously enforced—and also about the preconditions for civil disobedience.

CHAPTER 2

Cascades

I now examine how informational and reputational influences can produce social cascades—large-scale social movements in which many people end up thinking something, or doing something, because of the beliefs or actions of a few early movers. As in the case of conformity, participation in cascades is fueled by social influences. But where the idea of conformity helps to explain social stability, an understanding of cascades helps to explain social and legal movements, which can be stunningly rapid and also produce situations that are highly unstable. To get ahead of the story, the popularity of the *Mona Lisa*, William Blake, Jane Austen, Taylor Swift, and the Harry Potter novels is reasonably seen as the product of a cascade. The same is true for the success of Barack Obama, Donald Trump, and Brexit.

As preliminary evidence, consider a brilliant study of music downloads by the sociologist Duncan Watts and his coauthors.[1] Here's how the study worked. A control group was created in which people could hear and download one or more of seventy-two songs by new bands. In the control group, intrinsic merit was everything. Individuals were not told anything about what anyone else had downloaded or liked. They were left to make their own independent judgments about which songs they liked. To test the effect of social influences, Watts and his coauthors also created eight other subgroups. In each of these subgroups, people could see how many people had previously downloaded individual songs in their particular subgroups.

In short, Watts and his coauthors were exploring the relationship between social influences and consumer choices. What do you think happened? Would it make a small or a big difference, in terms of ultimate numbers of downloads, if people could see the behavior of others? The answer is that it made a huge difference. While the worst songs (as established by the control group) never ended up at the very top, and the best songs never ended up at the very bottom, *essentially anything else could happen.* If a song benefited from a burst of early downloads, it could do exceedingly well. If it did not get that benefit, almost any song could be a failure. As Watts and his coauthors later demonstrated, you can manipulate outcomes pretty easily, because popularity is a self-fulfilling prophecy.[2] If a site shows (falsely) that a song is getting downloaded a lot, that song can get a tremendous boost and eventually become a hit. John F. Kennedy's father, Joe Kennedy, was said to have purchased tens of thousands of early copies of his son's book, *Profiles in Courage.* The book became a bestseller.

With respect to the popularity of songs, Watts and his coauthors were exploring the effects of informational cascades. Their experiment showed that early popularity can have long-term effects, because people learn from what other people do and seem to like. As people learn from early popularity, they can make something into a huge hit, even if the same song would do poorly in another world in which the early listeners were unenthusiastic.

Cascades occur for judgments about facts and values as well as tastes. They operate within private and public institutions—small companies, large ones, the Catholic Church, labor unions, local governments, and national governments. And when people have affective connections with one another, the likelihood of cascades increases. In the area of social risks, cascades are especially common, with people coming to fear certain products and processes not because of private knowledge but because of the apparent fears of others.[3] The system of legal precedent also produces cascades, as early decisions lead later courts to a certain result, and eventually most or all courts come into line, not because of independent judgments but because of a decision to follow the apparently informed decisions of others.[4] The sheer level of agreement will be misleading if most courts have been influenced, even decisively influenced, by their predecessors, especially in highly technical areas.

By themselves, cascades are neither good nor bad. It is possible that the underlying processes will lead people to sound decisions about songs, cell phones, laptops, risks, morality, or law. The problem, a serious one, is that people may well converge, through the same processes, on erroneous or insufficiently justified outcomes. But to say this is to get ahead of the story; let us begin with the mechanics.

Informational Cascades: The Basic Phenomenon

In an informational cascade, people cease relying, at a certain point, on their private information or opinions. They decide instead on the basis of the signals conveyed by others. Once this happens, the subsequent statements or actions of few or many others add no new information. They are just following their predecessors. It follows that the behavior of the first few actors can, in theory, produce similar behavior from countless followers. A particular problem arises if people think the large number of individuals who say or do something are acting on independent knowledge; this can make it very hard to stop the cascade. Because so many people have done or said something—a politician is great, a product is dangerous, or someone is a criminal—people think to themselves, *How can they all be wrong?* The reality is that they can be, if they are mostly reacting to what others have said or done, and so are amplifying the volume of a signal by which they have themselves been influenced.

Here is a highly stylized illustration. Suppose that doctors are deciding whether to prescribe hormone therapy for menopausal women. If hormone therapy creates significant risks of heart disease, its net value, let us assume, is negative; if it does not create such risks, its net value is positive.[5] Let us also assume that the doctors are in a temporal queue, and all doctors know their place on that queue. From their own experiences, each doctor has some private information about what should be done. But each doctor also cares, rationally, about the judgments of others. Anderson is the first to decide, and prescribes hormone therapy if his judgment is low risk but declines if his judgment is high risk. Suppose that Anderson prescribes. Barber now knows that Anderson's judgment was low risk and that she too should certainly prescribe hormone therapy if she makes that independent judgment. But if her independent judgment is that the risk is high, she would—if she trusts Anderson no more and no less than she trusts herself—be indifferent about whether to prescribe and might simply flip a coin. Suppose that she really is not sure, and so she follows Anderson's judgment.

Now turn to a third doctor, Carlton. Suppose that both Anderson and Barber have prescribed hormone therapy but that Carlton's own information suggests that the risk is high. At least if he is not confident, Carlton might well ignore what he knows and prescribe the therapy. After all, both Anderson and Barber apparently saw a low risk, and unless Carlton thinks his own information is better than theirs, he should follow their lead. If he does, Carlton is in a cascade. To the extent that subsequent doctors know what others have done, and unless they too are confident, they will do exactly what Carlton did: *prescribe hormone therapy regardless of their private information*. "Since opposing information remains hidden, even a mistaken cascade lasts forever. An early preponderance toward either adoption or rejection, which may have occurred by mere coincidence or for trivial reasons, can feed upon itself."[6]

Notice that a serious problem here stems from the fact that for those in a cascade, actions do not disclose privately held information. In the example just given, doctors' actions will not reflect the overall knowledge of the health consequences of hormone therapy—even if the information held by individual doctors, if actually revealed and aggregated, would give a quite accurate picture of the situation. The reason for the problem is that individual doctors are following the lead of those who came before.

As noted, this problem is aggravated if subsequent doctors overestimate the extent to which their predecessors relied on private information and did not merely follow those who came before. If this is so, subsequent doctors might fail to rely on, and fail to reveal, private information that actually exceeds the information collectively held by those who started the cascade. As a result, the medical profession generally will lack information that it needs to have. Patients will suffer and possibly die. Importantly, participants in cascades act rationally in suppressing their private information, whose disclosure would benefit the group more than the individual who has it. The failure to disclose private information therefore presents a free-rider problem. To overcome that problem, some kind of reform seems to be necessary; it might involve changing institutional arrangements.

Of course, cascades do not always develop, and they usually do not last forever. Doctors used to believe in the "humors" (four distinct bodily fluids) and think that a deficiency in any one has harmful effects on health. They do not believe that now. Often people have, or think that they have, enough private information to reject the accumulated wisdom of others. Medical specialists often fall in this category. When cascades develop, they might be broken by corrective information, as has apparently happened in the case of hormone replacement therapy itself.[7] In the domain of science, peer-reviewed work provides a valuable safeguard.

But even among specialists and indeed doctors, cascades are common. "Most doctors are not at the cutting edge of research; their inevitable reliance upon what colleagues have done and are doing leads to numerous surgical fads and treatment-caused illnesses."[8] Thus an article in the prestigious *New England Journal of Medicine* explores "bandwagon diseases" in which doctors act like "lemmings, episodically and with a blind infectious enthusiasm pushing certain diseases and treatments primarily because everyone else is doing the same."[9] Some medical practices, including tonsillectomy and perhaps prostate-specific antigen (PSA) testing, "seem to have been adopted initially based on weak information," and extreme differences in tonsillectomy frequencies (and other procedures) provide good evidence that cascades are at work.[10] And once several doctors join the cascade, it is liable to spread. There is a link here with Muzafer Sherif's experiments, showing the development of divergent but entrenched norms, based on group processes in areas in which individuals lack authoritative information. In fact, prescriptions of hormone replacement therapy were fueled by cascade-like processes.[11]

What is true for doctors is highly likely to be true for lawyers, engineers, legislators, bureaucrats, judges, investors, and academics as well. It is easy to see how cascades might develop among groups of citizens, especially—but not only—if those groups are small, insulated, and connected by affective ties. If Barry does not know whether climate change is a serious problem, and if Alberta insists that it is not, Barry might well be persuaded, and their friend Charles is likely to go along, making it unlikely that Danielle will be willing to reject the shared judgment of the developing group. When small communities of like-minded people end up fearing a certain risk, or fearing and hating another group, cascades are often responsible.

Consider a legal analog, which offers lessons for those engaged in activities outside of law: There is a disputed issue under the Endangered Species Act. The question is what exactly the government has to do to protect endangered species. The stakes are high; environmental groups argue that the government has to do much more than the government is now doing. The first court of appeals to decide the question finds the issue genuinely difficult but resolves the issue favorably to the government. The second court of appeals tends to favor, very slightly, the view that the government is wrong, but the holding of the previous court of appeals is enough to tip the scales in the government's favor. A third court of appeals is also slightly predisposed to rule against the government, but it lacks the confidence to reject the shared view of two circuits. Eventually all circuits come into line, with the final few feeling the great weight of the unanimous position of others, and perhaps insufficiently appreciating the extent to which that weight is a product of an early and somewhat idiosyncratic judgment. Because the courts of appeals are in agreement, the Supreme Court refuses to get involved in the dispute. This can happen a lot—and it makes for bad law.

To be sure, precedential cascades do not always happen, and splits among courts of appeals are common.[12] One reason is that subsequent courts often have sufficient confidence to conclude that predecessor courts have erred. But it is inevitable that cascades will sometimes develop, especially in highly technical areas. It will be hard to detect them after they have occurred.

In terms of improving current practice, the implication is clear: judicial panels should be cautious about giving a great deal of weight to the shared view of two or more courts of appeals. A patient who seeks a second opinion should not disclose the first opinion to his new doctor; the goal is to obtain an independent view. In a similar vein, a court of appeals should be alert to the possibility that the unanimity of previous courts does not reflect independent agreement. And when the U.S. Supreme Court rejects the unanimous view of a large number of courts of appeals, it might be smart not to give undue weight to that unanimity; a precedential cascade could have been responsible for the consensus.[13] For the legal system, the danger is that a cascade, producing agreement among the lower courts, might prove self-insulating as well as self-reinforcing. Unless there is clear error, why should the Supreme Court become involved?

In informational cascades as discussed thus far, all participants are being entirely rational; they are acting as they should in the face of limited information. But as I have suggested, it is possible that participants in the cascade will fail to see the extent to which the decisions of their predecessors carry little independent information. If most people think that genetically modified foods create risks to health and the environment, can they really be wrong?

A possible answer is that they might indeed be wrong, especially if they are not relying on their private information and are following the signals sent by other people. And both outsiders and contributors to cascades often seem to mistake a cascade for a series of separate and independent judgments. Sometimes scientists, lawyers, and other academics sign petitions or statements, suggesting that hundreds and even thousands of people share a belief or an opinion. The sheer number of signatures can be extremely impressive. But it is perhaps less so if we consider the likelihood that most signatories lack reliable information on the issue in question and are simply following the apparently reliable but actually uninformative judgment of numerous others.

Even when those who participate in informational cascades are being entirely rational, there is a serious risk of error. People might converge on an erroneous, damaging, or dangerous path, simply because they are failing to disclose and to act on the basis of all the information that they have.

Cascades are easy to create in laboratory settings. Some of the experiments are detailed and a bit technical, but four general lessons are clear. First, people will often neglect their own private information and defer to the information provided by their predecessors. Second, people are alert to whether their predecessors are especially informed; more informed people can shatter a cascade. Third, and perhaps most intriguingly, cascade effects are greatly reduced if people are rewarded not for correct individual decisions but for correct decisions by a majority of the group to which they belong. Fourth, cascade effects, and blunders, are significantly increased if people are rewarded not for correct decisions but for decisions that conform to the decisions made by most people. As we shall see, these general lessons have implications for institutional design. They suggest that errors are most likely when people are rewarded for conforming and least likely when people are rewarded for helping groups and institutions to decide correctly.

The simplest experiment asked subjects to guess whether the experiment was using Urn A, which contained two red balls and one white, or Urn B, which contained two white balls and one red.[14] In each period, the contents of the chosen urn were emptied in a container. A randomly selected subject was asked to make one (and only one) private draw of a ball. After that draw, the subject recorded, on an answer sheet, the color of the draw and the subject's own decision about the urn. The subject's draw was not announced to the group, but the subject's decision about the urn was disclosed. Then the urn was passed to the next subject for another private draw, which was not disclosed, and for that subject's own decision about the urn, which *was* disclosed. This process continued until all subjects had made decisions, and at that time the experimenter announced the actual urn used. Subjects could earn $2 for a correct decision.

In this experiment, cascades often developed. After a number of individual judgments were revealed, people sometimes announced decisions that were inconsistent with their private draw but that fit with the majority of previous an-

nouncements.[15] More than 77 percent of "rounds" resulted
in cascades, and 15 percent of private announcements did
not reveal a "private signal," that is, the information provided
by people's own draw. Consider cases in which one person's
draw (say, red) contradicted the announcement of that person's predecessor (say, Urn B). In such cases, the second announcement nonetheless matched the first about 11 percent
of the time—far less than a majority but enough to ensure oc-
casional cascades. And when one person's draw contradicted
the announcement of two or more predecessors, the second
announcement was likely to follow those who went before.
Notably, the majority of decisions followed Bayes's rule and
hence were rationally based on available information[16]—but
erroneous cascades were nonetheless found. Here is an actual
example of a cascade producing an entertainingly inaccurate
outcome (the urn used was B):[17]

	1	2	3	4	5	6
Private draw	A	A	B	B	B	B
Decision	A	A	A	A	A	A

What is noteworthy here, of course, is that the total amount
of private information—four whites and two reds!—justified
the correct judgment, in favor of Urn B. But the existence
of two early signals, producing rational but incorrect judgments, led all others to fall in line. "Initial misrepresentative
signals start a chain of incorrect decisions that is not broken by more representative signals received later."[18] It should
be simple to see how this result might map onto real-world

assessments of factual, moral, and legal issues, especially in insulated groups where external correction is less likely.

How to Make and Break Cascades

Is the likelihood of cascades affected by institutional arrangements and social norms? Can social, political, or legal arrangements diminish or increase the risk of erroneous cascades, inadvertently or through conscious decision?

A central point here is that in an informational cascade, everyone is equal. People are simply trying to get the right answer, and they pay attention to the views and acts of others only because they want to be right. But it is easy to imagine slight alterations of the situation, so that some participants know more than others or so that people do not only care whether they are right. How would these alterations affect outcomes?

Fashion Leaders and Informed Cascade Breakers

In the real world of cascades, "fashion leaders" have unusual importance.[19] A prominent scientist might declare that immigration or climate change is a serious problem; a well-respected political leader might urge that a foreign country is run by killers or that war should be made against it; and a lawyer with particular credibility might conclude that some law violates the Constitution. In any of these cases, the speaker provides an especially loud informational signal, perhaps sufficient to start or to stop a cascade. In 2018,

Yale economist William Nordhaus won the Nobel Prize, largely for his work on climate change. Many people hoped that Nordhaus's increased prominence, courtesy of the prize, would fuel attention to the climate change problem.

Now turn to the actions of followers. In the hormone therapy case given above, none of the doctors is assumed to have, or believed to have, more information than his or her predecessors. But in many cases, people know, or think they know, a great deal. It is obvious that such people are far less likely to follow those who came before. Whether they will do so should depend on a comparison between the amount of information provided by the behavior of predecessors and the amount of private information that they have. And in theory, the most informed people will often shatter cascades, possibly initiating new and better ones. Whether this will happen, in practice, depends on whether the people who come later know, or believe, that the deviant agent was actually well informed. If so, the most informed people operate as fashion leaders.

A simple study attempts to test the question whether more informed people actually shatter cascades.[20] The study was essentially the same as the urn experiment just described, except that players had a special option after any sequence of two identical decisions (for example, two "Urn A" decisions): they could make not one but two independent draws before deciding (and thus obtain more information). The other subjects were informed of every case in which a player was making two draws. The simplest finding is that this "shattering mechanism" did indeed reduce the number of cascades—and thus significantly improved decisions.[21]

But the mechanism did not work perfectly. In some cases, cascades were nonetheless found. And in some cases, people who were permitted to draw twice, and saw two different balls (say, one red and one white), wrongly concluded that the cascade should be broken. The remarkable and somewhat disturbing outcome is that they initiated an inaccurate cascade. Consider this evidence, in a case in which the actual urn was A:

	1	2	3	4	5	6
Private draw	A	A	B, A	B	A	B
Decision	A	A	B	B	B	B

This disturbing pattern undoubtedly has real-world analogues, in which people sometimes give excessive weight to their own information, even if that information is ambiguous and if it makes sense to follow the crowd. But the larger point is the simple one: more informed people are less influenced by the signals of others, and they also carry more influence themselves.

But what about cases in which fashion leaders are not necessarily more informed or in which they are seen by others as having more information or more wisdom than they actually have? We can imagine self-styled experts—on diets, vaccines, herbal foods, alternative medicine, or economic trends—who successfully initiate cascades. They might be cranks, they might be crazy, or they might be self-promoters. The risk here is that their views will be wrongly taken as authoritative. On social media, that happens all the time. The result can be to lead people to errors and even to illness and death. "Fake news" can spread like wildfire; informational cascades are the culprits. In 2017 and 2018, that was a particular concern for Facebook, whose platform has often been used as a basis for the rapid transmission of falsehoods.

How can society protect itself? There are no panaceas here, but potential answers lie in good institutional arrangements, civil liberties, free markets, and good social norms, encouraging people to be skeptical of supposed truths. In systems with freedom of speech and free markets, it is always possible to debunk supposedly authoritative sources. And within groups, it is possible to structure decision-making to reduce the relevant risks. Votes might, for example, be taken in reverse order of seniority, to ensure that less experienced people will not be unduly influenced by the judgments of their predecessors; this is in fact the practice of the U.S. Supreme Court.

The spread of falsehoods on social media raises independent problems of course. For Facebook, an improved news feed can help; it might reduce the likelihood that damaging or intentional falsehoods will spread. (Facebook continues to test approaches to promote that goal.) Twitter might also experiment with initiatives designed to reduce the likelihood that damaging lies will go viral. It is worth considering whether to dismantle certain kinds of lies. But this is not the place for a treatment of possible reforms of social media.[22] The only point is that an understanding of the mechanisms behind informational cascades helps illuminate why social media can be so damaging to democracy.

Majority Rule: Rewarding Correct Outcomes by Groups Rather than by Individuals

How would the development of cascades be affected by an institution that rewards correct answers not by individuals but by the majority of the group? In an intriguing variation on the urn experiment, subjects were paid $2 for a correct group decision and penalized $2 for an incorrect group decision, with the group decision determined by majority rule.[23]

People were neither rewarded nor punished for correct individual decisions. The result was that only 39 percent of rounds saw cascades! In 92 percent of cases, people's announcement matched their private draw.[24] And because people revealed their private signals, the system of majority rule produced a substantial increase in fully informed decisions— that is, the outcomes that people would reach if they were somehow able to see all private information in the system. A simple way to understand this finding is to assume that a group has a large number of members and that each member makes an announcement that matches that member's private draw. As a statistical matter, it is overwhelmingly likely that the majority's position will be correct. As an example, consider this period from the majority rule experiment (the actual urn was A):[25]

	1	2	3	4	5	6	7	8	9
Private draw	A	A	A	A	B	A	A	A	B
Decision	A	A	A	A	B	A	A	A	B

What is the explanation for the significantly reduced level of cascade behavior in a system of majority rule? The answer lies in the fact that the individuals know they have nothing to gain from a correct individual decision and everything to gain from a correct group decision. As a result, it is in the individuals' interest to say exactly what they see, because it is the accurate announcement, from each person, that is most likely to promote an accurate group decision. That finding has large implications for how to structure groups and organizations.

Note that to explain the effect of majority rule in producing better outcomes, it is not necessary or even helpful to say that when people are rewarded for a correct group decision, they become altruistic or less concerned with their self-interest. On the contrary, self-interest provides a fully adequate explanation of the people's behavior. In the individual condition, it is perfectly rational to care little or not at all about whether one is giving an accurate signal to others. That signal is an "informational externality," affecting others, for better or for worse, but not affecting one's own likelihood of gain. If a subject's individual signal misleads others, the subject has no reason to care.

But under the majority rule condition that I have just described, rewarding accurate group decisions, the subject should care a great deal about producing an accurate signal, simply because an inaccurate signal will reduce the likelihood that the group will get it right. And here the subjects need not care about the accuracy of their individual decisions *except insofar as that decision provides a helpful signal to the group*. Hence it is only to be expected that cascades are reduced, and correct outcomes are increased, when people are rewarded for good group decisions.

There is a general point here. For most people, it is entirely rational, under plausible assumptions, to participate in a cascade. Participants benefit themselves even if they fail to benefit others (by failing to disclose privately held information) or affirmatively harm others (by giving them the wrong signal). This claim holds even if people are just trying to get it right and even if conformity is not rewarded as such. By contrast, it is not rational, under plausible assumptions, to disclose or act upon private information, even though the disclosure or action will actually benefit others. If other people have decided not to vaccinate their children, and if you think they must know what they are doing (even if you tend to disagree, based on what you know), you might just follow their lead and never voice your doubts.

The upshot is that dissenters, disclosing their own private information, need to be encouraged to speak out, simply because they confer benefits on those who observe them. The point applies to many organizations. And if the point is put together with an emphasis on the risk of cascades on courts, there is fresh reason to appreciate judicial dissents, if only because they increase the likelihood that majority decisions will receive critical scrutiny. Note here that within the U.S. Supreme Court alone, dissenting opinions have frequently become the law, indeed have become the law on well over 130 occasions—a point to which I will return.

This claim has an implication for appropriate institutional arrangements: any system that creates incentives for individuals to reveal information to the group is likely to produce better outcomes. A system of majority rule in which individuals know their well-being will be promoted (or not) depending on the decision of the group therefore has significant advantages. Well-functioning organizations, public as well as private, are likely to benefit from this insight. In this light, we might even offer a suggestion about the nature of civic responsibility: in case of doubt, citizens should reveal their private signal, rather than disguising that signal and agreeing with the crowd. Perhaps counterintuitively, this kind of behavior is not optimal from the point of view of the individual who seeks to get things right, but it is best from the point of view of a group or nation that seeks to use all relevant information.

It is important to make some distinctions here. The majority-rewarding variation on the urn experiment gives people an incentive to disclose accurate information that they have. This is the information from which the group benefits, and this is the information that does not emerge if people are rewarded for correct individual decisions. Full disclosure of accurate information is a central goal of institutional design. But the experiment does not suggest that a group is better off if people always disagree, or even if they always say what they think. In the tale of "The Emperor's New Clothes," the boy is not a skeptic or a malcontent. On the contrary, he is a particular kind of dissenter; he is a *discloser*, revealing the information that he actually holds. The majority-rewarding variation of the urn experiment encourages subjects to act like that boy.

By contrast, we can imagine a different kind of person, the *contrarian*, who thinks he will be rewarded, financially or otherwise, simply for disagreeing with others. There is no reason to celebrate the contrarian. In many cases, contrarians are unlikely to give any help to the group. If contrarians are known as such, their signals will be very noisy and not very informative. If contrarians are not known as such, they are often failing to disclose accurate information, simply because they are contrarians rather than disclosers; in that sense, they are not helping the group to arrive at correct decisions. We could imagine a variation on the urn experiment in which a contrarian confederate regularly announced the opposite of what his predecessor announced. It is safe to predict that such behavior would reduce cascades, but it would not reduce errors by individuals or groups. On the contrary, it would increase them.

Dissenters who are disclosers, then, are to be prized, at least if they are disclosing some important truth about the issue at hand. By contrast, dissenters who are contrarians are at best a mixed blessing. And we can also imagine dissenters who do not disclose a missing fact but instead simply state a point of view that would otherwise be missing from group discussion. Such dissenters might urge, for example, that a lot of immigration increases economic growth, that animals should have rights, that school prayer should be permitted, or that capital punishment should be banned. In the domains of politics and law, cascade-type behavior typically leads people to be silent not about facts but about points of view. It is obvious that groups need relevant facts; do they need to know about privately held opinions as well?

They certainly do, and for two different reasons. First, those opinions are of independent interest. If most or many people favor school prayer or believe that capital punishment is morally unacceptable, it is valuable to know that fact. Other things being equal, both individuals and governments do better if they know what their fellow citizens really think. Second, people with dissenting opinions might well have good arguments. Those arguments might depend, in the end, on judgments of fact; they might depend on purely normative claims. It is important for those who conform, fall into a cascade, or independently concur to hear those arguments. This is a standard Millian point,[26] to which I will shortly return.

On the federal courts in the United States, some judges suggest that they often offer a "go along concurrence," joining the majority though they privately disagree. Such judges give a false signal about their actual opinions and, very possibly, their future votes. That is true not only on federal courts. Many people offer "go-along concurrences," in companies, in legislatures, and in the White House. I was privileged to work for President Barack Obama, in the Executive Office of the President, and I saw some "go-along concurrences." When things were working best, people revealed what they thought.

Suppose, as is often the case, that people are rewarded not only or not mostly for being correct but also or mostly for doing what other people do. The reward might be material, in the form of more cash or improved prospects, or it might be nonmaterial, in the form of more and better relationships. In the real world, people are often punished for nonconformity and rewarded for conformity. People who reject the views of leaders or of the majority might well find themselves less likely to be promoted and more likely to be disliked. Organizations, groups, and governments often prize harmony, and nonconformists tend to introduce disharmony. Sometimes it is more important to be "on the team" than to be right. "Sometimes cultural groups adopt very high levels of norm enforcement that severely suppress the individual variations, innovations, and 'errors' that innate cultural transmission mechanisms require to generate adaptive evolutionary processes within groups."[27]

The likely result should be clear. If rewards come to those who conform, cascade-like behavior will increase, simply because the incentive to be correct is strengthened or replaced by the incentive to do what others do. The magnitude of this effect will depend on the size of the incentive to conform.

But whenever the incentive is positive, people will be all the more likely to ignore their private information and to follow others. The opposite result should be expected if people are penalized for following others or rewarded for independence; if so, cascade-like behavior should be reduced or even eliminated. I am now emphasizing the incentive to conform, but in some settings, independence is prized. I will offer a few remarks on that possibility below.

If conformity is rewarded, the problem is especially severe for the earliest disclosers or dissenters, who "may bear especially high costs because they are conspicuous, individually identified, and easy to isolate for reprisals."[28] And if the earliest dissenters are successfully deterred, dissent is likely to be exceedingly rare. Authoritarian governments are well aware of that fact; they try to nip dissent in the bud. But once the number of disclosers or dissenters reaches a certain level, there may be a tipping point, producing a massive change in behavior.[29] Indeed a single discloser, or a single skeptic, might be able to initiate a chain of events by which a myth is shattered.

Return to the tale of "The Emperor's New Clothes": "A child, however, who had no important job and could only see things as his eyes showed them to him, went up to the carriage. 'The Emperor is naked,' he said. . . . The boy's remark, which had been heard by the bystanders, was repeated over and over again until everyone cried: 'The boy is right! The Emperor is naked! It's true!'"[30] The power of the tale stems from its familiarity in ordinary life. All of us have seen situations in which someone says the emperor is naked or in which someone might (and should) have done so. The challenge is that it might be very difficult to initiate this process, especially if early disclosers are subject to social or legal sanctions.

Here we can see a potentially beneficial role of misfits and malcontents, who can perform a valuable function in getting otherwise neglected information and perspectives to others. Consider the suggestion that harmful obstacles to cultural improvement come from a "social structure" that eliminates "valuable innovators, experimenters, and error-makers from being viewed as people to copy."[31] The qualification, noted above, is that contrarians might help to reduce cascades without reducing errors.

With respect to conformity, these speculations are supported by an ingenious variation on the urn experiment mentioned above.[32] In this experiment, people were paid twenty-five cents for a correct decision but seventy-five cents for a decision that matched the decision of the majority of the group. There were punishments for incorrect and nonconforming answers as well. If people made an incorrect decision, they lost twenty-five cents. If their decision failed to match the group's decision, they lost seventy-five cents.

In this experiment, cascades appeared almost all of the time! No fewer than 96.7 percent of rounds resulted in cascades, and 35.3 percent of announcements did not match the announcer's private signal, that is, the signal given by his or her own draw. And when the draw of a subsequent person contradicted the announcement of the predecessor, 72.2 percent of people matched the first announcement. Consider, as a dramatic illustration, this period of the experiment (the actual urn for this period was B):[33]

	1	2	3	4	5	6	7	8	9	10
Private draw	A	B	B	B	A	B	B	B	A	B
Decision	A	A	A	A	A	A	A	A	A	A

The lesson is that institutions that reward conformity and punish deviance are far more likely to produce worse decisions and to reveal less in the way of private information. And here there is a link to the earlier suggestion that serious mistakes are committed by groups whose members are connected by bonds of affection, friendship, and solidarity. In such groups, members are usually less willing, or even unwilling, to state objections and counterarguments, for fear that these will violate generally held norms. Cascades and bad decisions are likely; return to the investment clubs discussed above. We can see here that an organization that depends on affective ties is likely to stifle dissent and to minimize the disclosure of private information and belief; some religious and political organizations are obvious illustrations. A socially destructive norm of conformity aggravates people's tendency to ignore their private information and to say and do what others do.

If an organization wants to avoid error, it should make clear that it welcomes the disclosure of private signals, simply because that is in the organization's own general interest. This point might seem counterintuitive, because in most well-functioning societies, conformity to the majority's view seems to be the civil thing to do. What I am suggesting here is that from the social standpoint, it is better to behave in the way that one would if being right were all that mattered and better still to behave as one would if a correct group decision were all that mattered.

Of course, the normative issues are not always simple. Bonds of affection and solidarity are often important to group members, and many people do not appreciate dissent and disagreement. Perhaps the real point of the relevant group or organization is not to perform well but to foster an optimistic outlook and good relationships. Conformists avoid creating the difficulties that come from contestation but at the expense, often, of a good outcome; dissenters tend to increase contestation while also improving performance.

In the abstract, it is not easy to specify the optimal trade-offs between the various goods. Everything depends on the group's goals—on what it is trying to maximize. If the only goal is to arrive at the right decisions, groups need to encourage disclosers and dissenters. If the central goal of group members is to maintain and improve social bonds or to have a good time, and not to carry out some task, conformity might be just fine, at least if nonconformists introduce tension and hostility. Or consider the question of dissent in wartime. It is important for those who wage war to know what citizens really think and also to have a sense of actual and potential errors. But it is also important, especially in wartime, for citizens to have a degree of solidarity, to be broadly optimistic, and to believe they are involved in a common endeavor; this belief can help solve collective action problems that otherwise threaten success. Some forms of dissent might correct mistakes while also weakening social bonds. Of course, freedom of speech should be the rule, but there is no simple solution to this dilemma. We might simply notice that those who are inclined to dissent must decide whether it is worthwhile to create the disruption that comes from expressing their views.

It is also possible that dissenters will be wrong, especially—but not only—if they are contrarians, and if they are wrong, they might spread errors through the same processes discussed here. They might be sources of fake news. Nothing in the discussion thus far shows that conformity and cascades are bad as such. The only suggestions have been that the underlying mechanisms increase the likelihood that people will not reveal what they know or believe and that this failure to disclose can produce social harm. It would not be difficult to generate experiments in which informational and reputational influences produce fewer mistakes than independence—if, for example, the task is especially difficult and if the experimenter introduces confident confederates equipped with the correct answer. When specialists have authority, and when people listen carefully to them, it is generally because errors are minimized through this route. But reputational influences carry serious risks insofar as they lead people, including specialists, not to disclose what they actually know. Indeed, this is the most troublesome implication of the conformity experiments.

When Silence Is Golden

I have been stressing cases in which disclosure is in the group's interest, but the discussion also suggests the opposite possibility, certainly when group members might go public and say what they know to the world at large.[34] Confidentiality can be essential. If group members reveal information that is embarrassing or worse, they might assist a competitor or an adversary. They might also make it harder for the group to have candid discussions in the future, simply because everyone knows that whatever is said might be made public. Strong norms against "leaking" are a natural corrective. And if some members of the group have engaged in wrongdoing, revelation of that fact might injure many or all group members.

Apart from confidentiality, anyone who has ever attended a workplace meeting is aware of the possibility that speakers receive the full benefits of the time they use, while inflicting costs on others. This unfortunate state of affairs can lead to unduly long meetings. The same problem can afflict the deliberations of both legislatures and courts. Conformity to a group norm, involving silence or informal time constraints, can be extremely valuable.

It is important to acknowledge that the problem I am emphasizing—the failure to disclose accurate information that will benefit the public—is closely paralleled by the problems raised in many cases in which silence, not revelation, is a collective good. And if disclosure will spread inaccurate information, it is unlikely to be beneficial, especially if it negates the beneficial effects of previous decisions or produces a cascade of its own (recall the spread of fake news). Because my focus is on the failure to disclose information, I will not devote attention to situations in which silence is golden, except to note that the basic analysis of those situations is not so different from the analysis here.[35]

The conformity experiment could itself be varied in many ways, with predictable results. If financial rewards were solely or almost solely for conformity, cascade behavior would be increased; if the seventy-five-cent reward were cut in half, cascade behavior should decline. Of course, it is possible to imagine many mixed systems. An obvious example is a system of majority rule in which people are not only rewarded when the group's majority reaches the right result but also rewarded for conformity or punished for nonconformity. Will cascades develop in such cases?

The answer will depend on the size of the two sets of incentives. If the accuracy of the group's decision will greatly affect individuals' well-being—if their lives will get much better as a result of good results—cascades are less likely. But if the ultimate outcome has little effect and if conformity will carry high rewards, cascades are inevitable. A system in which individuals receive two dollars for a correct majority decision and twenty-five cents for conforming will produce different (and better) results from a system in which individuals receive twenty-five cents for a correct majority decision and two dollars for conformity.

The real world of groups and democracy offers countless variations on these rewards, and often the rewards are highly indeterminate; people do not know what they are or have a hard time in quantifying them. But there can be little doubt that conformity pressures actually result in less disclosure of information. Consider the words of a medical researcher who questions a number of Lyme disease diagnoses: "Doctors can't say what they think anymore. . . . If you quote me as saying these things, I'm as good as dead."[36] When privately interviewed, gang members express considerable discomfort about their antisocial behavior, but their own conduct suggests a full commitment, leading to a widespread belief that most people approve of what is being done.[37] Or consider the remarks of a sociologist who publicly raised questions about the health threats posed by mad cow disease, suggesting that if you raise those doubts publicly, "you get made to feel like a pedophile."[38]

Alexis de Tocqueville explained the decline of the French church in the mid-eighteenth century in these terms: "Those who retained their beliefs in the doctrines of the Church . . . dreading isolation more than error, professed to share the sentiments of the majority. So what was in reality the opinion of only a part . . . of the nation came to be regarded as the will of all and for this reason seemed irresistible, even to those who had given it this false appearance."[39] Or consider, as a chilling example, the suggestion from a killer of Mostar during the Bosnian war that his actions were not a product of his convictions about the evil character of those he was killing. On the contrary, many of them were his former friends. His explanation was that he had to do what he did to remain a part of his Serbian community.[40]

There is a final wrinkle. In the settings discussed thus far, dissenters proceed at their peril and nonconformity is punished. This will be my emphasis throughout. But in some contexts, dissenters might be attempting to improve their own prospects, and dissenting might be a sensible way of doing that. Dissenters may be self-serving, and they may be trying to spur their stalled careers. It happens all the time. People who run a website might become popular because of their iconoclastic or even wild views. A political dissenter, challenging some widespread practice, sometimes becomes more prominent and more successful as a result. Judges who dissent in high-profile cases might not greatly fear that their reputation will be harmed; they might think the dissent will redound to their benefit.

The point is strengthened once we consider the fact that a nation consists of countless communities with a wide range of values and beliefs. Public dissenters might impair their reputation in one group but simultaneously strengthen it in another. On a radio show, on Facebook, or on Twitter, they might be saying, "Look at me!" And if people look at them, they might be able to advance in some way that matters to them. Of course, some people say and do exactly what they think and do not greatly care about their reputations; they want to add information. They are rebels with a cause.

But return to my main concern. Too much of the time, people do not want to lose the good opinion of relevant others, and the result of this desire is to reduce the information that the public obtains. Apart from information, people might have preferences and values. They might believe that new immigrants should be welcomed. They might believe in animal rights. But in either case they might not reveal what they think, simply because of the pressure to conform. I have suggested that from the standpoint of democratic practice, this is a problem as well. Most of the time, it is valuable for people to disclose what they want and what they value. The basic findings, as in the urn experiments, would undoubtedly be the same for preferences and values as well as facts, with rewards for conformity greatly increasing the apparent (not real) degree of agreement.

This point helps explain why "unpopular or dysfunctional norms may survive even in the presence of a huge, silent majority of dissenters."[41] Fearing the wrath of others, people might not publicly contest practices and values that they privately abhor. The practice of sexual harassment long predated the idea of sexual harassment, and the innumerable women who were subject to harassment did not like it. But too much of the time they were silent, partly because they feared the consequences of public complaint. It is interesting to speculate about the possibility that many current practices fall in the same general category: those that produce harm, and are known to produce harm, but persist because most of those who are harmed believe they will suffer if they object in public.

Reputational Cascades

If conformity pressures are taken seriously, we can see the possibility of reputational cascades, parallel to their informational sibling.[42] In a reputational cascade, people think they know what is right, or what is likely to be right, but they nonetheless go along with the crowd. Even the most confident people sometimes fall prey to this process, silencing themselves in the process. In fact, the conformity-rewarding version of the urn experiment is an elegant example of a reputational cascade. It is thus possible to exploit the influence of peer pressure, found in the conformity experiments, to show how many social movements become possible.

Suppose that Albert suggests that genetically modified foods are a serious problem and that Barbara concurs publicly with Albert, not because she actually agrees with Albert but because she does not wish to seem, to Albert, to be ignorant or indifferent to human health and environmental protection. If Albert and Barbara agree that genetically modified foods are a serious problem, Cynthia might not contradict them publicly and might even seem to share their judgment, not because she believes the judgment to be correct but because she does not want to face the hostility or lose the good opinion of others. It is easy to see how this process might generate a cascade. Once Albert, Barbara, and Cynthia offer a united front on the issue, their friend David might be most reluctant to contradict them even if he thinks they are wrong. We could use the same stylized facts to describe enthusiasm for current political leaders, a stated belief that all is going well in the workplace, and an apparent commitment to any particular ideology.

In the actual world of group decisions, people are of course uncertain whether publicly expressed statements are a product of independent knowledge, participation in an informational cascade, or reputational pressure. It is reasonable to think that much of the time, listeners and observers overstate the extent to which the actions of others are based on independent information.

Reputational cascades occur in the private sector. They happen within companies, within nonprofits, and within religious organizations. They also arise within all branches of government. Of course legislators are vulnerable to reputational pressures. That is part of their job. When elected representatives suddenly support legislation to deal with an apparent (sometimes not real) crisis, they are involved in a reputational cascade. Consider, for example, the rush in the United States, in July 2002, to enact measures to deal with corporate corruption.[43] Undoubtedly many legislators had private qualms about the very legislation they supported, and some of them probably disapproved of measures for which they nonetheless voted. I do not mean to take a stand on the relevant legislation. Perhaps it was a terrific idea. The only point is that the widespread support was a product, in part, of a reputational cascade.

As a more vivid example, consider the unanimous (!) disapproval, by members of the U.S. Senate, of the court of appeals decision to strike down the use of the words "under God" in the Pledge of Allegiance.[44] In both cases, some legislators were involved in a reputational cascade, repressing their private doubts in order to avoid injury to their reputations.

I have emphasized that in an informational cascade, the most serious problem is that the group fails to receive privately held information. Exactly the same problem arises in a reputational cascade, where members of the group or the public are also unable to learn what many people know and think. Here people silence themselves not because they believe they are wrong but because they do not want to face the disapproval that, they think, would follow from expressing the view they believe to be correct. The problem and the result are *pluralistic ignorance*: ignorance, on the part of most or all, of what most people actually think.[45] In the face of pluralistic ignorance, people can assume, wrongly, that others have a certain view, and they alter their statements and actions accordingly.

Under certain conditions, this self-censorship is an extremely serious social loss. For example, Communism was long able to sustain itself in Eastern Europe not only because of force but also because people believed, wrongly, that most people supported the existing regime.[46] The fall of Communism was made possible only by the disclosure of privately held views, which turned pluralistic ignorance into something closer to pluralistic knowledge. As we shall see, self-censoring can undermine success during war. Reputational pressures also help fuel ethnic identifications, sometimes producing high levels of hostility among groups for which, merely a generation before, such identifications were unimportant and hostility was barely imaginable. And if certain views are punished, unpopular views might eventually be lost to public debate, so that what was once "unthinkable" is now "unthought."[47] Views that were originally taboo, and offered rarely or not at all, become excised entirely, simply because they have not been heard. Here too those who do not care about their reputation, and who say what they really think, perform a valuable public service, often at their own expense.

Various civil liberties, including freedom of speech, can be seen as an effort to insulate people from the pressure to conform, and the reason is not only to protect private rights but also to protect the public against the risk of self-silencing. A memorable claim by the philosopher Joseph Raz clarifies the point: "If I were to choose between living in a society which enjoys freedom of expression, but not having the right myself, or enjoying the right in a society which does not have it, I would have no hesitation in judging that my own personal interest is better served by the first option."[48] The claim makes sense in light of the fact that a system of free speech confers countless benefits on people who do not much care about exercising that right. Consider the fact that in the history of the world, no society with democratic elections and free speech has ever experienced a famine[49]—a demonstration of the extent to which political liberty protects people who do not exercise it.

Freedom of association is especially noteworthy here, because it allows people to band together in groups in which the ordinary incentive to conform might be absent or even reversed. Society in general might punish certain political views, but associations can be found in which those views are tolerated or even encouraged. Many movements have been made possible in that way, including the movements for sex equality, environmentalism, religious liberty, and the American Revolution itself. The secret ballot can be seen in related terms. One advantage of the secret ballot is that it reduces informational pressures, leading voters to express their own preferences and to be less influenced by the views of others. (Recall the majority-rewarding version of the urn experiment.) But the more obvious advantage is that the voters can act anonymously and cast their ballots without fear of opprobrium.

Just as informational cascades may be limited in their reach, there can be *local reputational cascades*—those that reshape the public pronouncements of particular subgroups without affecting those of the broader society. When certain subgroups believe that some dishonorable political cause is very important, that nonexistent risks are actually quite serious, or that some hopeless medical treatment produces miracle cures, local reputational cascades might well be involved, simply because local skeptics do not speak out. On Facebook, local reputational cascades happen every day.

Of course informational influences interact with reputational ones. A few decades ago, for example, South Africa experienced the literally deadly phenomenon of "AIDS denial," with prominent leaders suggesting that AIDS is not a real disease but instead a conspiracy to sell certain drugs to poor people. In that case, a cascade did develop, but it was based mostly on transmission of alleged facts (fake news),

not on fear of reputational harm.[50] But if we emphasize reputational pressures, we can identity an important reason for
the persistence of unusual and baseless beliefs—about facts
and values—among various communities of like-minded
people. It is often tempting to attribute such differences to
deep historical or cultural factors, but the real source, much
of the time, is reputational pressure.

Political leaders often play an important role in building
that pressure. If leaders insist that something is true or that
the nation should pursue a certain course of action, some
citizens might well be reluctant to dissent, if only because of
a fear of public disapproval. Here as elsewhere, the result can
be serious social loss. And here again a strong system of civil
liberties, and an insistence on making a safe space for enclaves of dissenters, can be justified not as an effort to protect
individual rights but as a safeguard against social blunders.
A market system aggregates and spreads information better
than any planner could possibly do.[51] In the same way, a system of free expression and dissent protects against the false
confidence and the inevitable mistakes of planners, both private and public.

It would make little sense to say that cascades, in general,
are good or bad. Sometimes cascade effects will overcome
group or public torpor, by generating concern about serious
though previously ignored problems. Sometimes cascade
effects will make people far more worried than they would
otherwise be and produce large-scale distortions in private
judgments, public policy, and law. The antislavery movement
had distinctive cascade-like features, as did the environ-

mental movement in the United States, the fall of Communism, the anti-apartheid movement in South Africa, and the #MeToo movement of 2017 and 2018; so too with Mao's Cultural Revolution and the rise of Nazism in Germany. Typically, cascades are quite fragile, precisely because people's commitments are based on little private information. What I have emphasized here is the serious risk that social cascades can lead to widespread errors, factual or otherwise.

Boundedly Rational Cascades

Thus far the discussion has assumed that people are largely rational—that they take account, rationally, of the information provided by the statements and actions of others and that they care, sensibly enough, about their reputation. The principal exception, suggested above, is that people may mistake a cascade for a large number of independent decisions. But it is well known that human beings are "boundedly rational." In most domains, people use heuristics, or mental shortcuts, and they also show identifiable biases.[52] Indeed, following others can itself be seen as a heuristic, one that usually works well but that also misfires in some cases. And for other heuristics and for every bias, there is a corresponding possibility of a cascade.

Consider, for example, the availability heuristic, which has probably become the most well known in public policy and law.[53] When people use the availability heuristic, they answer a hard question about probability by asking whether examples come readily to mind. How likely is a flood, an earthquake, an airplane crash, a traffic jam, a terrorist attack, or a disaster at a nuclear power plant? Lacking statistical knowledge, people try to think of illustrations. For people without statistical knowledge—which is to say most people—it is hardly irrational to use the availability heuristic. The problem is that this heuristic can lead to serious errors of fact, in the form of excessive fear of small risks and neglect of large ones. And indeed both surveys and actual behavior show extensive use of the availability heuristic. Whether people will buy insurance for natural disasters is greatly affected by recent experiences.[54] If floods have not occurred in the immediate past, people who live on flood plains are far less likely to purchase insurance. In the aftermath of an earthquake, insurance for earthquakes rises sharply—but it declines steadily from that point, as vivid memories recede.

For present purposes, the key point is that the availability heuristic does not operate in a social vacuum. Whether an incident is "available" is a function of social interactions. These interactions rapidly spread salient illustrations within relevant communities, making those illustrations available to many or most. Sometimes the processes are intensely local. Should swimmers worry about shark attacks? Do immigrants commit a lot of crimes? Does gun control save lives? Are young girls likely to be abducted? In all of these cases, the United States has seen "availability cascades,"[55] in which salient examples were rapidly spread from one person to the next. Availability cascades are equally common elsewhere; in the first decades of the twenty-first century, Russia, Germany, France, Italy, and Mexico experienced many of their own.

Note that this process typically involves information. If some people use a recent assault to show there is a serious risk of crime ten blocks north, or a recent airplane accident to show that it is unsafe to fly, their statements carry a certain authority, leading others to believe they are true. And in the case of shark attacks, violent crime by immigrants, and abduction of young girls, the media spread a few gripping examples, apparently providing information that was rapidly transmitted to millions of people. But reputational forces play a role as well. Much of the time, people are reluctant to say that an example is misleading and hence that others' fears are groundless. Efforts at correction may suggest stupidity or callousness, and a desire to avoid public opprobrium may produce a form of silencing.

Availability cascades are ubiquitous. Vivid examples, alongside social interactions, help account for decisions to purchase insurance against natural disasters. Cascade effects explain the existence of widespread public concern about abandoned hazardous waste dumps (a relatively trivial environmental hazard). Availability cascades have spurred public fears not only of shark attacks, immigration, and abductions of girls but also of the pesticide Alar, plane crashes, and school shootings. Such effects helped produce massive dislocations in beef production in Europe in connection with "mad cow disease"; they help also to account for the outpouring of fear of Ebola in the United States and Europe during the second decade of the twenty-first century. They certainly spurred the #MeToo movement in Sweden, the United States, and elsewhere.

My suggestion is not that in all or most of these cases, availability cascades led to excessive or inappropriate reactions. On the contrary, such cascades sometimes have the valuable effect of promoting public attention to serious but neglected problems. The suggestion is only that the intensity of public reactions is best understood by seeing the interaction between the availability heuristic and the cascade effects I have been emphasizing. The problem is that those interactions make some errors inevitable, simply because a heuristic, even if generally helpful, is bound to misfire in many cases. Here as elsewhere, dissent can be an important corrective. For organizations and governments, the question is how to make dissent less costly, or even to reward it, especially when dissenters benefit not themselves but others.

CHAPTER 3

Group Polarization

Thus far I have been exploring how informational and reputational influences produce conformity and cascades. I have also identified factors that can increase or reduce the likelihood of both of these. When people are not bound by affective ties, the magnitude of social influences diminishes. When people define themselves in opposition to the relevant others—if "we" are opposed to a "they"—conformity effects might be greatly reduced. Because of "reactive devaluation," there might be no conformity at all. Greater confidence about the facts can reduce conformity, and when people know that certain people are more informed, cascades can be shattered.

With these points in view, let us now turn to the phenomenon of group polarization, a phenomenon that contains large lessons about the behavior of interest groups, private companies, religious organizations, political parties, juries, legislatures, judicial panels, and even nations.

The Basic Phenomenon

What happens within deliberating bodies? Do groups compromise? Do they move toward the middle of the tendencies of their individual members? The answer is now clear, and it is perhaps not what intuition would suggest: members of a deliberating group typically end up in a more extreme position in line with their tendencies before deliberation began.[1] This is the phenomenon known as group polarization. Group polarization is the usual pattern with deliberating groups, having been found in hundreds of studies involving more than a dozen countries, including the United States, France, and Germany.[2] Each of the three studies with which I began—involving deliberating citizens, deliberating juries, and deliberating judges—involved group polarization.

It follows that a group of people who think immigration is a serious problem will, after discussion, think that immigration is a horribly serious problem; that those who dislike the Affordable Care Act will think, after discussion, that the Affordable Care Act is truly awful; that those who approve of an ongoing war effort will, as a result of discussion, become still more enthusiastic about that effort; that people who dislike a nation's leaders will dislike those leaders quite intensely after talking with one another; and that people who disapprove of the United States, and are suspicious of its intentions, will increase their disapproval and suspicion if they exchange points of view.

Indeed, there is specific evidence of the latter phenomenon among citizens of France.[3] When like-minded people talk with one another, they usually end up thinking a more extreme version of what they thought before they started to talk. It should be readily apparent that enclaves of people, inclined to rebellion or even violence, might move sharply in that direction as a consequence of internal deliberations. Political extremism is often a product of group polarization.[4]

There is a close relationship between group polarization and cascade effects. Both of these are a product of informational and reputational influences. A key difference is that group polarization refers to the effects of deliberation,[5] and cascades need not involve discussion at all. In addition, group polarization does not necessarily involve a cascade-like process. Polarization can result simply from simultaneous independent decisions, by all or most individuals, to move toward a more extreme point in line with the tendencies of group members.

In the United States, group polarization helped both Barack Obama and Donald Trump to ascend to the presidency. Speaking mostly with one another, Obama supporters and Trump supporters become intensely committed to their candidate. On Facebook and Twitter, we can see group polarization in action every hour, every minute, or every day. As enclaves of like-minded people proliferate online, group polarization becomes inevitable. Sports fans fall prey to group polarization; so do companies deciding whether to launch some new product.

To see the operation of group polarization in a legal context, let us explore in more detail the study of punitive intentions and punitive damage awards, referred to in the introduction.[6] The details are somewhat technical. I recite them here because they tell us something about the dynamics of *outrage*, which is often a source of both private and public action. The study involved about three thousand jury-eligible citizens. Its major purpose was to determine how individuals would be influenced by seeing and discussing the punitive intentions of others. Hence subjects were asked to record, in advance of deliberation, a "punishment judgment" on a scale of 0 to 8, where 0 indicated that the defendant should not be punished at all and 8 indicated that the defendant should be punished extremely severely. After the individual judgments were recorded, jurors were sorted into six-person groups and asked to deliberate to a unanimous "punishment verdict." It would be reasonable to predict that the verdicts of juries would be the median of punishment judgments of jurors, but the prediction would be badly wrong.

Instead, the effect of deliberation was to create both a severity shift for high-punishment jurors and a leniency shift for low-punishment jurors.[7] When the median judgment of individual jurors was four or more on the eight-point scale, the jury's verdict was above that median judgment. Consider, for example, a case involving a man who nearly drowned on a defectively constructed yacht. Jurors tended to be outraged by the idea of a defectively built yacht, and groups were significantly more outraged than their median members.

But when the median judgment of individual jurors was below four, the jury's verdict was typically below that median judgment. Consider a case involving a shopper who was injured in a fall when an escalator suddenly stopped. Individual jurors were not greatly bothered by the incident, seeing it as a genuine accident rather than a case of serious wrongdoing, and juries were more lenient than individual jurors. Here, then, is a clear example of group polarization in action. Groups whose members were antecedently inclined to impose large punishments become inclined toward larger punishments. The opposite effect was found with groups whose members were inclined toward small punishments.

Outrage

When we consider the ingredients of punishment judgments, this finding has a large implication for people's behavior both inside and outside the courtroom. Punishment judgments are rooted in outrage,[8] and a group's outrage, on a bounded numerical scale, is an excellent predictor of the same group's punishment judgments on the same scale.[9] Apparently people who begin with a high level of outrage become still more outraged as a result of group discussion. Moreover, the degree of the shift depends on the antecedent level of outrage; the higher the original level, the greater the shift as a result of internal deliberations.[10] There is a point here about the wellsprings of not only severe punishment by jurors, mobs, and governments but also rebellion and violence. If like-minded people, predisposed to be outraged, are put together with one another, significant changes are to be expected. The American Revolution was made possible in this way, and the same is true for the revolts against apartheid and Communism.

It should be easy to see that group polarization is at work in feuds, ethnic and international strife, and war. One of the characteristic features of feuds is that members of feuding groups tend to talk only to one another, fueling and amplifying their outrage and solidifying their impression of the relevant events. Group polarization occurs every day within

Israel and among the Palestinian Authority. Many social movements, both good and bad, become possible through the heightened effects of outrage; consider the movement for rights for deaf people, which was greatly enhanced by the fact that the deaf have a degree of geographical isolation.[11] Social enclaves are breeding grounds for group polarization, sometimes for better and sometimes for worse.

Hidden Profiles and Self-Silencing in Groups

The tendency toward extreme movement is the most noteworthy finding in the literature on group polarization. But there is another point, of special importance for my argument here: in a deliberating group, those with a minority position often silence themselves or otherwise have disproportionately little weight. The result can be "hidden profiles"—important information that is not shared within the group.[12] Group members often have information but do not discuss it, and the result is to produce inferior decisions.

Consider a study of serious errors within working groups, both face-to-face and online.[13] The purpose of the study was to see how groups might collaborate to make personnel decisions. Résumés for three candidates, applying for a marketing manager position, were placed before the groups. The attributes of the candidates were rigged by the experimenters so that one applicant was clearly the best for the job described. Packets of information were given to subjects, each containing a subset of information from the résumés, so that each group member had only part of the relevant information.

The groups consisted of three people, some operating face-to-face, some operating online.

Two results were especially striking. First, group polarization was common, as groups ended up in a more extreme position in accordance with the original thinking of their members. Second, almost none of the deliberating groups made what was conspicuously the right choice, because they failed to share information in a way that would permit the group to make an objective decision. Members tended to share positive information about the winning candidate and negative information about the losers, while also suppressing negative information about the winner and positive information about the losers. Their statements served to "reinforce the march toward group consensus rather than add complications and fuel debate."[14]

This finding is in line with the more general suggestion that groups tend to dwell on shared information and to neglect information that is held by few members. It should be unnecessary to emphasize that this tendency can lead to large errors. To understand this particular point, it is necessary to explore the mechanisms that produce group polarization.

Why Polarization?

Why do like-minded people go to extremes? There are three main answers, involving information, corroboration, and social comparison.[15]

The most important answer, involving informational influences, is similar to what we have seen in connection with conformity and cascades. The simple idea here is that people respond to the arguments made by other people—and the "argument pool," in any group with some initial disposition in one direction, will inevitably be skewed toward that disposition.[16] A group whose members tend to think that Israel is the real aggressor in the Middle East conflict will tend to hear many arguments to that effect and relatively few opposing views. It is almost inevitable that the group's members will have heard some, but not all, of the arguments that emerge from the discussion. Having heard all of what is said, people are likely to move further in the anti-Israel direction. So too with a group whose members tend to oppose immigration: group members will hear a large number of arguments against immigration and a smaller number of arguments on its behalf.

If people are listening, they will have a stronger conviction, in the same direction from which they began, as a result of deliberation. An emphasis on limited argument pools also helps to explain the problem of "hidden profiles" and the greater discussion of shared information during group discussion. It is simply a statistical fact that when more people have a piece of information, there is a greater probability that it will be mentioned.[17] Hidden profiles are a predictable result, to the detriment of the ultimate decision.

The second answer points to the relationships among confidence, corroboration, and extremism.[18] The intuition here is simple: people who lack confidence, and who are unsure what they should think, tend to moderate their views. It is for this reason that cautious people, not knowing what to do, are likely to choose the midpoint between relevant extremes.

But if other people seem to share your view and corroborate your beliefs, you are likely to become more confident that you are correct—and hence to move in a more extreme direction. You might think that on a scale of 1 to 10, the likelihood that climate change is occurring is 7—but if most people in your group agree that climate change is occurring, you might move up to 9.

In a wide variety of experimental contexts, people's opinions have been shown to become more extreme simply because their view has been corroborated and because they have been more confident after learning of the shared views of others.[19] Note that there is an obvious connection between this explanation and the finding, mentioned above, that a panel of three judges of the same party is likely to behave quite differently from a panel with only two such judges. The existence of unanimous confirmation from two others will strengthen confidence and hence strengthen extremity.[20]

The third answer, involving social comparison, begins with the claim that people want to be perceived favorably by other group members and also to perceive themselves favorably.[21] Their views may, to a greater or lesser extent, be a function of how they want to present themselves. Once people hear what others believe, they adjust their positions in the direction of the dominant position, to hold onto their preserved self-presentation. They may want to signal, for example, that they are not cowardly or cautious, especially in an entrepreneurial group that disparages these characteristics, and hence they will frame their position so they do not appear as such by comparison to other group members. And when they hear what other people think, they might find they occupy a somewhat different position, in relation to the group, from what they hoped, and they shift accordingly.

For example, if people believe they are somewhat less opposed to immigration than most people, they might shift a bit after finding themselves in a group of people who are strongly opposed to immigration, to maintain their preferred self-presentation. The phenomenon appears to occur in many contexts. People may wish, for example, not to seem too enthusiastic, or too restrained in their enthusiasm for, affirmative action, feminism, or an increase in national defense; hence their views may shift when they see what other group members think. The result is to press the group's position toward one or another extreme and also to induce shifts in individual members. There is a great deal of support for this account of group polarization.[22]

Note that an emphasis on social comparison gives a new and perhaps better explanation for the existence of hidden profiles and the failure to share certain information within a group. People might emphasize shared views and information, and downplay unusual perspectives and new evidence, simply from a fear of group rejection and a desire for general approval.[23] In political and legal institutions, there is an unfortunate implication: group members who care about one another's approval, or who depend on one another for material or nonmaterial benefits, might well suppress highly relevant information. Hence this account of group polarization is connected with the idea of reputational cascades, where blunders are highly probable.

Skewed Debates

In the context of punitive damage awards by juries, a particular finding deserves emphasis. Thus far my discussion of the relevant study has stressed how deliberation affected punitive intentions, measured on a bounded numerical scale. But jurors were also asked to record their monetary judgments, in advance of deliberation, and then to deliberate to monetary verdicts. Did high awards go up and low awards go down, as the idea of group polarization might predict?

Not quite. The principal effect was to make nearly *all* awards go up, in the sense that the jury's monetary award typically exceeded the median award of individual jurors.[24] Indeed, the effect was so pronounced that in 27 percent of cases, the jury's verdict was as high as, or higher than, the highest predeliberation judgment of jurors![25]

There is a further point. The effect of deliberation in increasing dollar awards was most pronounced in the case of high awards. For example, the median individual judgment, in the case involving the defective yacht, was $450,000, whereas the median jury judgment, in that same case, was $1,000,000. But awards shifted upward for low awards as well.

Why did this happen? A possible explanation, consistent with group polarization, is that any positive median award suggests a predeliberation tendency to punish, and deliberation aggravates that tendency by increasing awards. But even if it is right, this explanation seems insufficiently specific. The striking fact is that those arguing for higher awards seem to have an automatic *rhetorical advantage* over those arguing for lower awards. A subsequent study of law students supports this claim, suggesting that given existing social norms, people find it easy, in the abstract, to defend higher punitive awards against corporations and harder to defend lower awards.[26] The basic idea is that even if you know absolutely nothing about the facts of a controversy, you might find it easy to come up with arguments in favor of more severe punishment—for example, to give a strong deterrent signal or to reflect the outrage of the community. And you might find it harder to come up with arguments in favor of smaller awards. Whenever social norms are in place, they might make it easier to produce arguments in favor of a particular side—which might mean that deliberating groups will naturally tend to move in the direction of that side.

Findings of rhetorical advantage have been made in seemingly distant areas. Suppose that doctors are deciding what steps to take to resuscitate patients. Are individuals less likely to support heroic efforts than groups? Evidence suggests that as individuals, individual doctors are less likely to do so than groups, apparently because those who favor such efforts have a rhetorical advantage over those who do not.[27] The underlying dynamics are intriguing, and here is a speculation about how they work. Individual doctors do some kind of cost-benefit calculation, and they are willing to say that all things considered, heroic efforts are not a terrific idea. But when they are in groups, individual doctors start to feel a bit ashamed about cost-benefit calculations, and they lean in the direction of trying to save the patient. Norms favor that kind of leaning.

Or consider the difference between individual behavior and team behavior in the Dictator Game, used by social scientists to study selfishness and altruism.[28] In this game, a subject is told that she can allocate a sum of money, say $10, between herself and some stranger. The standard economic prediction is that most subjects will keep all or almost all of the money for themselves; why should we share money with strangers? But the standard prediction is wrong. Most people choose to keep somewhere between $6 and $8 and to share the rest.[29] That is interesting enough, but the question here is how individual behavior is affected once people are placed in teams.

The answer is that team members choose still more equal divisions.[30] This result seems best explained by reference to a rhetorical advantage disfavoring selfish behavior, even within a group that stands to benefit from selfishness. Apparently, people do not want to appear to be greedy in front of fellow group members. Of course this outcome, and the effect of group influence, would change if the team in the Dictator Game had some reason to be hostile to the beneficiaries of their generosity. We can easily imagine a variation of the Dictator Game in which, for example, people of a relatively poor and embattled religious group were deciding how much to allocate to another religious group that was thought to be both hostile and far wealthier. In this variation, the rhetorical advantage might favor greater selfishness.

What produces a rhetorical advantage? The simplest answer points to prevailing social norms, which of course vary across time and place. Among most Americans, current norms make it easier to argue, other things equal, for higher penalties against corporations for egregious misconduct. But it is possible to imagine subcommunities (corporate headquarters?) in which the rhetorical advantage runs the other way. In any case it is easy to envisage many other contexts in which one or another side has an automatic rhetorical advantage.

Consider, as possible examples, debates over whether there should be higher penalties for those convicted of drug offenses, whether more refugees should be allowed into one's country, whether more money should be spent on national defense, or whether tax rates should be reduced. In modern political debates, those favoring higher penalties and lower taxes often have the upper hand. Of course there are limits on the feasible level of change. But when a rhetorical advantage is involved, group deliberation will produce significant shifts in individual judgments. Undoubtedly legislative behavior is affected by mechanisms of this sort, and it is likely that many movements within judicial panels can be explained in similar terms.

Are rhetorical advantages unhelpful or damaging? In the abstract, this is an impossible question to answer, because shifts have to be evaluated on their merits. Perhaps the higher punitive awards that follow deliberation are simply better. So too, perhaps, for the movements by doctors, taking more heroic measures, and by groups deciding how equally to spread funds. The only point is that such advantages exist, and it would be most surprising if they were always benign.

More Extremism, Less Extremism

Group polarization is not a social constant. It can be increased or decreased, and even eliminated, by certain features of group members or their situation.

First, extremists are especially prone to polarization. It is more probable that they will shift, and it is probable that they will shift more. When they start out at an extreme point and are placed in a group of like-minded people, they are likely to go especially far in the direction with which they started.[31] There is a lesson here about the sources of terrorism and political violence in general. And because there is a link between confidence and extremism, the confidence of particular members also plays an important role; confident people are both more influential and more prone to polarization.[32]

Second, if members of the group think they have a shared identity and a high degree of solidarity, there will be heightened polarization.[33] One reason is that if people feel united by some factor (for example, politics or religious convictions), dissent will be dampened. If individual members tend to perceive one another as friendly, likable, and similar to them, the size and likelihood of the shift will increase.[34] The existence of affective ties reduces the number of diverse arguments and also intensifies social influences on choice. One implication, noted above, is that mistakes are likely to be increased when group members are united mostly through bonds of affection and not through concentration on a particular task; it is in the former case that alternative views will be less likely to find expression. Hence people are less likely to shift if the direction advocated is being pushed by unlikable or unfriendly group members.[35] A sense of "group belongingness" affects the extent of polarization.[36] In the same vein, physical spacing tends to reduce polarization; a sense of common fate and intragroup similarity tend to increase it, as does the introduction of a rival "outgroup."[37]

An interesting experiment attempted to investigate the effects of group identification.[38] Some subjects were given instructions in which group membership was made salient (the "group immersion" condition), whereas others were not (the "individual" condition). For example, subjects in the group immersion condition were told that their group consisted solely of first-year psychology students and that they were being tested as group members rather than as individuals. The relevant issues involved affirmative action, government subsidies for the theater, privatization of nationalized industries, and the phasing out of nuclear power plants.

The results were striking. Polarization generally occurred. But there was the least polarization in the individual condition; polarization was far greater in the group immersion condition, when group identity was emphasized. This experiment strongly suggests that polarization is highly likely to occur, and to be most extreme, when group membership is made salient. Political activists of all kinds are often aware of the fact; so are many entrepreneurs.

Third, over time, group polarization can be fortified because of "exit," as members leave the group because they reject the direction in which things are heading.[39] If exit is pervasive, the tendency to extremism will be greatly aggravated. The group will end up smaller, but its members will be both more like-minded and more willing to take extreme measures. That very fact will mean that internal discussions will produce more extremism still. If the strongest loyalists are the only people who stay, the group's median member will be more extreme, and deliberation will produce increasingly extreme movements.

Fourth, when one or more people in a group know the right answer to a factual question, the group is likely to shift in the direction of accuracy.[40] If the question is how many people were on the earth in 1940, or where the Olympics were held in 2004, or the distance between Berlin and Paris, and if one or a few people know the right answer, the group is likely not to polarize but to converge on that answer. The reason is simple: the person who knows the answer will speak with confidence and authority and is likely to be convincing for that very reason.

Of course this is not inevitable. Solomon Asch's conformity experiments show that social pressures can lead to errors even with respect to simple factual claims. But in many cases, group members who are ignorant will be tentative, and members who are informed will speak confidently. This is enough to ensure convergence on truth rather than polarization. Here there is a link between what prevents polarization and what shatters cascades: a person who knows, and is known to know, the truth.

In this light, it becomes easier to understand the outcomes of experiments that show a potential advantage of groups over individuals.[41] One set of experiments involved two analytic tasks. The first involved a statistical problem, requiring subjects to guess the composition of an urn containing blue balls and red balls. (This experiment involved team decision-making and was not a test for cascade effects.) The other involved a problem in monetary policy, asking participants to manipulate the interest rate to steer the economy.

People were asked to perform as individuals and in groups. The basic results for the two experiments were similar. Groups significantly outperformed individuals (and they did not, on balance, take longer to make decisions). Perhaps most surprisingly, there were no differences between group decisions made with a unanimity requirement and group decisions made by majority rule.

How can these results be explained? The experimenters do not have a complete account. An obvious possibility is that each group contained one or more strong analysts, who were able to move the group in the right direction. But a series of regressions, comparing the performance of the best individual players, offers only mixed support for this hypothesis.[42] It seems that in these experiments, group results were driven by the best points and arguments, which would be spread among the various individual players. Here we find a tribute to the widespread belief that groups can do much better than individuals.

Fifth, depolarization might be found when the relevant group consists of individuals drawn equally from two extremes.[43] Thus if five people who initially favor caution are put together with five people who initially favor risk-taking, the group judgment might move toward the middle. Consider a study consisting of six-member groups specifically designed to contain two subgroups (of three persons each) initially committed to opposed extremes; the effect of discussion was to produce movement toward the center.[44] One reason may be the existence of information and persuasive arguments in both directions.[45]

Interestingly, this study of equally opposed subgroups found the greatest depolarization with obscure matters of fact (e.g., the population of the United States in 1900)—and the least depolarization with highly visible public questions (e.g., whether capital punishment is justified). Matters of personal taste depolarized a moderate amount (e.g., preference for basketball or football, or for colors for painting a room).[46] Hence "familiar and long-debated issues do not depolarize easily."[47] With respect to such issues, people are simply less likely to shift at all, in part "because the total pool of arguments has long been familiar to all,"[48] and nothing new will emerge from discussion.

These findings suggest a separate point: group members might not shift at all when they begin with strong convictions. If you put together a group of people who love Brexit with a group of people who hate Brexit, they might end up just where they started.

Consider in this regard an experiment designed to see how group polarization might be dampened.[49] The experiment involved the creation of four-person groups, which, on the basis of pretesting, were known to include equal numbers of persons on two sides of political issues (whether smoking should be banned in public places, whether sex discrimination is a thing of the past, and whether censorship of material for adults infringes on human liberties). Judgments were registered on a scale running from +4 (strong agreement) to 0 (neutral) to −4 (strong disagreement).

In half of the cases (the "uncategorized condition"), subjects were not made aware that the group consisted of equally divided subgroups in pretests. In the other half (the "categorized condition"), subjects were told that they would find a sharp division in their group, which consisted of equally divided subgroups. They were also informed who was in which group and told that they should sit around the table so that one subgroup was on one side facing the other group. In the uncategorized condition, discussion generally led to a dramatic reduction in the mean gap between the two sides, thus producing a convergence of opinion toward the middle of the two opposing positions (a mean of 3.40 scale points, on the scale of +4 to −4).

But things were very different in the categorized condition. Here the shift toward the median was much less pronounced. Frequently there was barely any shift at all (a mean of 1.68 scale points). In short, calling attention to group membership made people far less likely to shift in directions urged by people from different groups.

My discussion of group influences—of conformity, cascades, and polarization—is now complete. I have emphasized many findings from social science, but I have tried at the same time to give a sense of how those findings bear on issues in law and politics. It should be clear that there is a long list of potential applications, and any set of selections from that list is inevitably arbitrary. In the discussion that follows, I emphasize four areas in which an understanding of group influences helps to illuminate legal problems.

The first involves law's expressive function—the circumstances in which a mere statement, made by the law, is likely to affect people's behavior. I draw a link among legal pronouncements, Milgram's experimenter, and Asch's unanimous confederates. The second involves the institutions of the U.S. Constitution, based on the founding enthusiasm for the expression of diverse and dissenting views. I suggest that the U.S. Constitution creates a deliberative democracy of a distinctive kind—a deliberative democracy that prizes heterogeneity.

The third area involves the value of dissent in a place not always thought to benefit from it: the federal judiciary. Because judges are subject to conformity and cascade effects as well as group polarization, it is exceedingly important to promote ideological diversity within the federal courts. The fourth and final area involves affirmative action in higher education. Focusing generally on the significance of *cognitive* diversity, I offer an ambivalent lesson, suggesting that racial diversity is, in some domains, unimportant for the exchange of (relevant) ideas, but that it can be important in other domains, sometimes in both undergraduate and law school education.

CHAPTER 4

Law and Institutions

Many people have been interested in law's expressive function—in the role of law in "making statements," as opposed to regulating conduct directly through actual punishments for violations.[1] In this chapter, I make three suggestions. First, we can better understand the expressive function of law if we see certain legal enactments as offering signals about good behavior and about what other people think is good behavior. Second, a legal expression is most likely to be effective if violations of the law are highly *visible*; visibility matters because people do not want to incur the wrath of others. Third, a legal expression is less likely to be effective if violators are part of a deviant subcommunity that rewards, or at least does not punish, noncompliance. In such cases, behavior within the subcommunity can counteract the effects of law.

Each of these points can be closely connected with an understanding of conformity, cascades, and group polarization. We can thus use that understanding to see when government might bring about compliance without relying on public enforcement—and also when enforcement is likely to be indispensable.

Law as Signal

Sometimes law is infrequently enforced, but there is automatic or near-automatic compliance.[2] It is in this sense that law seems to have an expressive function, making statements and having effects merely by virtue of those statements. When such effects occur, it is because the law offers signals on both the informational and the reputational sides. If law is made by sensible people, and if it bans certain conduct, there is a good reason to presume that the conduct should be banned. And when law bans certain conduct, there is good reason to presume that other people think the conduct should be banned. In either case, sensible people have fresh reason to do what the law asks them to do.

Of course the presumptions can be rebutted. Informed people might know that the law is asking people to do something senseless or not to do something sensible. They might also know that most people, or most relevant people, actually reject the law. But if these cases are the exception rather than the rule, we can have a better understanding of why law will produce movement even if no one is enforcing it.

Consider, for example, an empirical study of bans on smoking in public places.[3] The simplest lesson is that people comply with those bans even though they are hardly ever enforced. The study finds that in three cities in California—Berkeley, Richmond, and Oakland—the authorities heard very few complaints about violations. In Berkeley, the responsible health department officials found it unnecessary to issue even a single formal citation, and no cases were referred for prosecution. In restaurants in Richmond, compliance was nearly 100 percent, with workplace compliance hovering between 75 and 85 percent. The level of compliance was also extremely high in Oakland, with the exception of "certain restaurants in the Asian community where nearly all the patrons are smokers."[4] High levels of compliance were also found in workplaces, high schools, and fast-food restaurants. Other studies, conducted in Cambridge, Massachusetts, and Winnipeg, Manitoba, similarly find that bans on public smoking are almost entirely self-enforcing.[5]

This evidence suggests that a legal pronouncement can have the same effect as Solomon Asch's unanimous confederates. When a law bans smoking in public places, the pronouncement carries information to the effect that it is wrong, all things considered, to smoke in public places. Equally important, the law suggests that most people believe it is wrong to smoke in public places. And if most people think it is wrong to smoke in public places, would-be smokers are less likely to smoke, in part because they do not want to be criticized or reprimanded. Importantly, would-be smokers also know that those who would reprimand them would have the law on their side. They would not merely be confronted by people who dislike being around smokers. Those who confront them would be able to say that smokers are violating the law.

It follows that when law is effective but unenforced, an important reason is the possibility of private enforcement. If violations have a high degree of visibility, and if violators risk the wrath of private enforcers, compliance is likely to become widespread. "In contrast to violations of laws against driving and drinking, narcotics use, and tax evasion, infractions of no-smoking rules in public places are relatively visible . . . to an almost omnipresent army of self-interested, highly motivated private enforcement agents—nonsmokers who resist exposure to tobacco smoke."[6] In some cases, the law might even be equivalent to Stanley Milgram's experimenter, with a significant degree of authority even if no sanctions will be imposed. To the extent that the experimenter's authority comes from a perception of knowledge and expertise, the law is closely analogous.

We might think of the underlying laws as exercises in *norm management*—and extremely inexpensive ones at that. They are inexpensive in the sense that taxpayer resources may be unnecessary to produce compliance. And in the best cases, expressive law might even start, shatter, or fuel a cascade. Once compliance begins and is widely seen as such (especially from "fashion leaders"), there might well be *compliance cascades*, spurred by both informational and reputational influences. In the context of sexual harassment and smoking, law does seem to have caught a wave—and to have enlarged it significantly (though not nearly enough).[7]

A key point here is that the law was ahead, but not too far ahead, of the public at large. If the law were not ahead of the public, it would add nothing and in that sense have no effect at all. But if the law moved too far ahead of the public, it could not be effective without aggressive enforcement activity. And a law that is too far ahead of the public is unlikely, for that very reason, to be aggressively enforced; prosecutors and jurors are unlikely to punish people when the public does not support punishment. Law may be most effective when it goes beyond existing social values but remains close enough that it can claim to draw on them.

Thus far I have emphasized the situation from the point of view of the would-be violator. But a law has effects on private enforcers as well. In the absence of a legal ban, people who object to smoking in public places might well be timid about complaining, even if they find cigarette smoke irritating or worse. The same people are likely to be energized by a supportive enactment, which suggests both that they are right and that their beliefs are generally shared. With law on their side, they are less likely to appear to be noisy intermeddlers invoking a parochial norm. They can point to a kind of violation. People who complain about speeding, drunk driving, sexual harassment, or smoking in public are far more likely to believe they have a legitimate complaint if the law requires the behavior they seek. Equally important, they are more likely to think that other people will believe they have a legitimate complaint. That can embolden them.

Now of course this is not all of the picture. Among some people, the law has a high degree of moral authority, greatly exceeding the shared but unenacted view of many people. If this is the case, the law's authority will extend well beyond that of Asch's unanimous confederates and probably beyond that of Milgram's experimenter as well. But we cannot fully appreciate law's moral authority without seeing it as intertwined with the informational and reputational factors that I have been emphasizing.

The Preconditions of Norm Management

When will norm management work without significant enforcement activity? When will it fail? Begin with the case of a rational person who is considering whether to comply with the law. Among the relevant considerations are (a) the likelihood of enforcement; (b) the magnitude of the punishment in the event of enforcement; (c) the reputational costs of violation; (d) the reputational benefits of violation; (e) the intrinsic benefits of compliance (perhaps a refusal to smoke will have health benefits); and (f) the intrinsic costs of compliance (perhaps it is extremely pleasant to smoke and extremely unpleasant not to smoke). By adjusting any of the variables over which it has control, government might be able to achieve greater compliance. For present purposes, my emphasis is on (c) and (d). I have referred to the case of smoking, but we could use any number of examples: driving while drunk, texting while driving, discriminating on the basis of age, using unlawful drugs, or stealing.

To know whether a legal pronouncement will be effective, a key point involves the nature and extent of private enforcement. Recall that in the Asch experiments, the level of error is significantly decreased when people's answers are given anonymously and also when people are given a financial incentive to answer correctly. These findings suggest that seemingly modest changes in social context counteract the pressure to conform. Consider in this light the close empirical association between visibility and compliance without enforcement. Parking in places reserved for the handicapped and smoking in public are easy to see, and in both cases private enforcement is likely. Drivers do not much like it when nonhandicapped people park in places reserved for the handicapped. By contrast, tax violations and sex offenses tend to be invisible, and hence violators need not worry so much, at the time of violation, about the risk of public opprobrium.

To know whether there will be compliance, it is important to specify the signal sent by compliance and noncompliance. The mere enactment of law can alter the signal that accompanies people's conduct. For example, enactment of law might make an actor's conduct seem honorable where it previously seemed cowardly or accusatory or otherwise provided a socially damaging signal. Consider, for example, a teenager who wants to buckle his seatbelt but fails to do so because he does not want to signal his cowardice. A law that requires people to buckle their belts can make a decision to buckle a reflection of compliance with law, rather than a generalized fear. A law that forbids people from driving and drinking, or from texting while driving, might be effective for similar reasons.

In short, the mere existence of the law can alter the "meaning" of compliance, to suggest that those who comply are simply law abiders. Similarly, those who violate the law, under the new circumstances, are no longer courageous but instead (technically) criminals. We can imagine circumstances in which this shift actually increases the level of violations. Some people like to be rebels, and if they violate the law, all the better. But in most communities most of the time, the legal enactment—the statement made by the law—will tend to shift behavior in the desired direction. Consider here the behavioral finding that if people are informed of a social norm, they tend to comply with it. This finding has been applied to increase tax compliance, to reduce use of illegal drugs, and even to encourage doctors to reduce excessive opioid prescriptions.[8]

At the same time, law's expressive function can be reduced or even counteracted if there is private support for violations. "People will defy dominant norms or laws, despite considerable risks of punishment, when they enjoy the social support of a 'deviant subculture' that continues to endorse the validity of condemned behavior."[9] In such cases, prospective violators are roughly in the position of peer-supported subjects in the Milgram experiment—at least if they have strong reason, based on principle or self-interest, not to comply. If you are a smoker or a drug user, surrounded by smokers or drug users, you might continue to smoke or to use drugs, even if the law prohibits you from doing so. And if the law is perceived as senseless, private support for violations can operate in the same way as a voice of reason in the Asch experiments.

Hence it is possible to find "deviant subcultures" in which violations of law are effectively rewarded, through admiration and even a general increase in stature. It is also possible to find subcultures in which those who comply with the law can be heavily "taxed," through ridicule, ostracism, or even violence. Drug use is the most obvious example; gang violence sometimes occurs simply because it is expected and rewarded by peers. Laws that are infrequently enforced will, in such communities, be highly ineffective, because private enforcement is lacking, and indeed private forces push hard against compliance. It is even possible to imagine *noncompliance cascades*; such cascades can involve information, as people witness the violations of prominent others, perhaps including dissident "fashion leaders." They can also involve reputation, as people learn that in the relevant community, there will be no loss in the good opinion of others, and possibly some gain, for violations.

In this light, it is easy to see why there is a great deal of compliance with legal bans on parking in handicapped spaces and on smoking in public places, whereas there is far less compliance with legal bans on certain sexual behavior and (in certain domains) the Internal Revenue Code. And it is also possible to understand the phenomenon of civil disobedience. When those engaged in civil disobedience are able to reach a critical mass, the relevant law (perhaps it calls for racial segregation) loses its authority, both as evidence of what should be done and as evidence of what (reasonable) people think should be done. The authority of the law is overcome by the authority of those who disobey the law. Here conformity pressures, cascade effects, and group polarization strongly favor disobedience.

How might government handle the troublesome situations in which violations are both invisible and widespread? One possible remedy would be to let people know (if it is true) about high levels of voluntary compliance. Because people like to do what others do, large effects can come from reminders that most people obey the law or avoid harmful conduct. In fact, there is evidence that taxpayers are far more likely to comply with the tax law if they believe that most people pay their taxes voluntarily and far less likely to do so if they believe that noncompliance is widespread.[10] A similar example may be drawn from college campuses. Students with a penchant for "binge drinking" tend to believe that the number of binge drinkers is higher than it actually is. When informed of the actual numbers, they are less likely to persist in their behavior.[11] These examples suggest that an understanding of group influences, and of the information conveyed by the acts of others, might be enlisted in efforts to reduce conduct that is unlawful or otherwise dangerous to self and others.

Let us now turn to issues of institutional design. As we have seen, the likelihood and consequences of conformity, cascades, and group polarization very much depend on institutional choices. Recall in particular that people are far more likely to reveal their own information if they are rewarded for a correct group decision rather than for a correct individual decision.

I begin with a brief note on the relationship between dissent and war, with the suggestion that conformity, and suppression of dissent, can undermine military preparedness. I also explore some of the institutions of the U.S. Constitution, suggesting that the founders' largest theoretical contribution consisted in their enthusiasm for diversity and the "jarring" of diverse views in government. Turning to contemporary issues, I discuss the role of group influences on federal judges and the dispute over "diversity" as a justification for affirmative action in higher education.

Dissent and War

We have seen that an understanding of social influences increases appreciation of the social role of whistleblowers and dissenters, many of whom sacrifice their own self-interest and simultaneously benefit the public. Perhaps the most general point here involves the role of diversity and dissent within democratic institutions. Consider the account of Luther Gulick, a high-level official in the Roosevelt administration during World War II. In 1948, shortly after the Allied victory, Gulick delivered a series of lectures, unimaginatively titled "Administrative Reflections from World War II," which offered, in some detail, a set of observations about bureaucratic structure and administrative reform.[12] In a brief epilogue, Gulick set out to compare the war-making capacities of democracies with those of their Fascist adversaries.

Gulick began by noting that the initial evaluation of the United States, among the leaders of Germany and Japan, was "not flattering."[13] The United States was, in their view, "incapable of quick or effective national action even in [its] own defense because under democracy [it was] divided by [its] polyglot society and under capitalism deadlocked by [its] conflicting private interests."[14] The adversaries of the United States said that it could not fight, and they believed what they said. And dictatorships did seem to have real advantages. They were free of delays, inertia, and sharp internal divisions. They did not have to reckon with the opinions of a mass of citizens, some with little education and little intelligence.

Dictatorships could rely on a single leader and an integrated hierarchy, making it easier to develop national unity and enthusiasm, to master surprise, and to act vigorously and with dispatch. But these claims about the advantages of totalitarian regimes turned out to be "bogus."[15]

The United States and its allies performed far better than Germany, Italy, and Japan. Gulick linked their superiority directly to democracy itself and in particular "to the kind of review and criticism which democracy alone affords."[16] In a totalitarian regime, plans "are hatched in secret by a small group of partially informed men and then enforced through dictatorial authority."[17] Such plans are likely to contain fatal weaknesses. By contrast, a democracy allows wide criticism and debate, thus avoiding "many a disaster."

In a totalitarian system, criticisms and suggestions are neither wanted nor heeded. "Even the leaders tend to believe their own propaganda. All of the stream of authority and information is from the top down," so that when change is needed, the high command never learns of that need. But in a democracy, "the public and the press have no hesitation in observing and criticizing the first evidence of failure once a program has been put into operation."[18] In a democracy, information flows within the government—between the lowest and highest ranks—and via public opinion. Of course dissent can be muted in wartime, and for reasons I have discussed, this muting is a mixed blessing. If everyone seems to be on the same page, morale may be strengthened. But if disagreement is reduced, beneficial ideas—involving the nature, scope, justice, and wisdom of war—may be absent.

With a combination of melancholy and surprise, Gulick noted that the United States and its allies did not show more unity than Germany, Japan, and Italy. "The gregarious social impulses of men around the world are apparently much the same, giving rise to the same reactions of group loyalty when men are subjected to the same true or imagined group threats."[19] Top-down management of mass morale, by the German and Japanese leaders, actually worked. Dictatorships were less successful in the war, not because of less loyalty or more distrust from the public but because leaders did not receive the checks and corrections that come from democratic processes.

Gulick is offering a claim here about how institutions perform better when challenges are frequent, when people do not stifle themselves, and when information flows freely. Of course Gulick is providing his personal account of a particular set of events, and we do not really know if success in war is a product of democratic institutions. The Soviet Union, for example, fought valiantly and well, even under the tyranny of Stalin. But Gulick's general theme contains a great deal of truth. Institutions are far more likely to succeed if they contain mechanisms that subject leaders to critical scrutiny and if they ensure that courses of action will be subject to continuing monitoring and review from outsiders—if, in short, they use diversity and dissent to reduce the risks of error that come from social influences.

Constitutional Design

These points very much bear on the design of the U.S. Constitution, which attempts to create a deliberative democracy, that is, a system that combines accountability to the people with a measure of reflection and reason-giving. In recent decades, many people have discussed the aspiration to deliberative democracy. Their goal has been to show that a well-functioning system attempts to ensure not merely electoral responsiveness but also an exchange of reasons in the public sphere. The emphasis on reason-giving can be seen as a rebuke to purely populist accounts of democracy, which suggest that majorities should rule, regardless of the justifications they give for what they would like to do. Deliberative democrats are acutely aware of the risks of conformity, cascades, and group polarization. They want to protect liberty as well as self-government.

In a deliberative democracy, the exercise of public power must be justified by reasons, not merely by the will of some segment of society and indeed not merely by the will of the majority. Both the opponents and the advocates of the U.S. Constitution were firmly committed to political deliberation. They also considered themselves "republicans," committed to a high degree of self-government. But deliberative democracies can come in many different forms. The framers' greatest innovation consisted not in their belief in deliberation, which was uncontested at the time, but in their fear of homogeneity, their enthusiasm for diversity, and their effort to accommodate and to structure that diversity. In the founding period, a large part of the nation's discussion turned on the feasibility of maintaining a deliberative democracy—a republic—in a nation with its heterogeneous citizenry.

The antifederalists, opponents of the proposed Constitution, thought that this was impossible. Thus Brutus, an especially articulate advocate of the antifederalist view, spoke for the classical tradition when he urged, "In a republic, the manners, sentiments, and interests of the people should be similar. If this be not the case, there will be constant clashing of opinions; and the representatives of one part will be continually striving against those of the other."[20]

The advocates of the Constitution believed that Brutus had it exactly backward. They welcomed the diversity and the "constantly clashing of opinions" and affirmatively sought a situation in which "the representatives of one part will be continually striving against those of the other." Alexander Hamilton spoke most clearly on the point, urging that the "differences of opinion, and the jarring of parties in [the legislative] department of the government . . . often promote deliberation and circumspection; and serve to check the excesses of the majority."[21] From the standpoint of political deliberation, the central problem is that widespread error and social fragmentation are likely to result when like-minded people, insulated from others, move in extreme directions simply because of limited argument pools and parochial influences. A constitution that ensures the "jarring of parties" and "differences of opinion" will provide safeguards against unjustified movements of view. The authors of the U.S. Constitution had an intuitive understanding of group polarization and cascade effects, because they had observed both of these before, during, and after the revolutionary period.

A similar point emerges from one of the most illuminating early constitutional debates, raising the question of whether the Bill of Rights should include a "right to instruct" representatives. That right was defended with the claim that citizens of a particular state ought to have the authority to bind their representatives about how to vote. This defense might seem plausible as a way of improving the political accountability of representatives—and so it seemed to many people at the time. But there is a problem with this view, especially in an era in which political interest was closely aligned with geography. In such an era, it is likely that the citizens of a particular state, influenced by one another's views, might end up with indefensible positions, very possibly as a result of its own insularity, leading to cascade effects and group polarization. In rejecting the right to instruct, Roger Sherman gave the decisive argument:

> The words are calculated to mislead the people, by conveying an idea that they have a right to control the debates of the Legislature. This cannot be admitted to be just, because it would destroy the object of their meeting. I think, when the people have chosen a representative, it is his duty to meet others from the different parts of the Union, and consult, and agree with them on such acts as are for the general benefit of the whole community. If they were to be guided by instructions, there would be no use in deliberation.[22]

Sherman's words reflect the founders' general receptivity to deliberation among people who are quite diverse and who disagree on issues both large and small. Indeed, it was through deliberation among such persons that "such acts as are for the general benefit of the whole community" would emerge.

Most important, the institutions of the U.S. Constitution reflect a fear of conformity, cascade effects, and group polarization. To combat the risks, the document creates a range of checks on ill-considered judgments that emerge from those processes. An obvious example is bicameralism, designed as a safeguard against a situation in which one house—in the framers' view, most likely the House of Representatives—would be overcome by short-term passions and even group polarization. This was the point made by Hamilton in endorsing a "jarring of parties" within the legislature. James Wilson's great lectures on law spoke of bicameralism very much in these terms, referring to "instances, in which the people have become the miserable victims of passions, operating on their government without restraint," and seeing a "single legislature" as prone to "sudden and violent fits of despotism, injustice, and cruelty."[23]

To be sure, a cascade can cross the boundaries that separate the Senate from the House; such crossings do occur. But their different compositions and cultures provide a significant safeguard against warrantless cascades. Here the Senate was thought to be especially important. Consider the widely reported story that on his return from France, Thomas Jefferson called George Washington to account at the breakfast table for having agreed to a second chamber. "'Why,' asked Washington, 'did you pour that coffee into your saucer?' 'To cool it,' quoth Jefferson. 'Even so,' said Washington, 'we pour legislation into the senatorial saucer to cool it.'"[24]

We can understand many aspects of the system of checks and balances in the same general terms. The separation of powers itself reduces the likelihood that cascade effects, or group polarization, will lead the government in terrible directions. Because law cannot be brought to bear against citizens without the concurrence of the legislative and executive branches, enacting and then enforcing the law, there is a strong safeguard against oppression. The president might favor some law and argue vigorously on its behalf, but the legislature might refuse to enact it. In addition, the duty to present legislation to the president for his or her signature protects against cascade effects within the legislative branch; the president has the authority to veto legislation of which he or she disapproves. Even if the legislature enacts an oppressive or foolish law, the president might refuse to enforce it. And even if the legislature enacts it and the president enforces it, courts might intervene, perhaps by declaring it unconstitutional.

Federalism itself was, and remains, an engine of diversity, creating "circuit breakers" in the form of a variety of sovereigns with separate cultures. In the federal system, social influences may produce error in some states, and states can certainly fall into cascades. But the existence of separate systems creates some check on the diffusion of error. One state might do something terrible, but if so, its citizens can flee to other states. The very fact that citizens can "exit" provides a safeguard against oppressive or foolish enactments. The right to leave is a safeguard against tyranny, stupidity, and oppression, often created by conformity, cascades, and polarization.

Judicial power itself was understood in related terms, quite outside of the context of constitutional review. Consider Hamilton's account:

> But it is not with a view to infractions of the Constitution only that the independence of judges may be an essential safeguard against the effects of occasional ill humours in the society. These sometimes extend no farther than to the injury of the private rights of particular classes of citizens, by unjust and partial laws. Here also the firmness of the judicial magistry is of vast importance in mitigating the severity and confining the operation of such laws. It not only serves to moderate the immediate mischiefs of those which may have been passed, but it operates as a check upon the legislative body in passing them; who, perceiving that obstacles to the success of an iniquitous intention are to be expected from the scruples of the courts, are in a manner compelled by the very motives of the injustice they mediate, to qualify their attempts.[25]

Of course the Constitution's explicit protection of freedom of speech and its implicit protection of freedom of association help to ensure spaces for diversity and dissent. In that way, they counteract some of the risks of mistake that stem from social influences. For present purposes, the analysis of free speech is straightforward, but it is worth emphasizing that freedom of expression allows a nation's citizens to monitor its leaders and thus to call them to account. It enables the nation's boys and girls to say that the emperor has no clothes. It authorizes informed people, confident that they are right, to disclose what they know. There is no panacea here against widespread error, but there is a lot of help.

James Madison, the author of the first amendment, invoked ideas of this kind to object to the whole idea of a "Sedition Act," criminalizing certain forms of criticism of public officials. Madison urged that "the right of electing the members of the Government constitutes . . . the essence of a free and responsible government" and that the "value and efficacy of this right depends on the knowledge of the comparative merits and demerits of the candidates for the public trust."[26] If group influences are kept in mind, one implication is that both private and public institutions have a legitimate interest in introducing diversity of opinion into domains that otherwise consist of like-minded people. The reason is simply to diminish the risks of error. If modern technologies allow people to sort themselves into echo chambers, there is a risk that people will be insulated from competing views. Perhaps government should be entitled to respond. Of course any such efforts, on government's part, will introduce first amendment problems of its own.[27]

Freedom of association presents some important wrinkles. As we have seen, an understanding of group polarization suggests that associational freedom can produce significant risks, above all because like-minded people might, by the laws of social interactions, go in unjustifiably extreme directions. Society might well become fragmented as a result of "iterated polarization games," in which groups of like-minded people—initially different, but not terribly different, from one another—drive their members toward increasingly diverse positions. Many nations are now seeing such iterated polarization games (sometimes spurred by social media), and they make governance far more difficult. Small differences in initial views can be magnified, through social interactions, into very large ones. An advantage of this process is that it serves to increase society's total stock of "argument pools," but across groups, it also increases the likelihood of mutual suspicion, misunderstanding, and even hatred.

At the same time, freedom of association helps to counteract the informational and reputational influences that lead people to fail to disclose information, preferences, and values. By allowing a wide diversity of communities, imposing pressures of quite different kinds, freedom of association increases the likelihood that at some point, important information will be disclosed and eventually spread.

Nothing in this brief account means that the U.S. Constitution, as originally ratified or as now understood, contains the ideal institutions and rights for balancing diversity with other goals, including stability. Some people argue on behalf of proportional representation,[28] either of demographic groups or of a large number of parties, and it is possible to understand those arguments as responsive to the goal of guaranteeing a wide range of ideas in government. In some nations, there have been serious attempts to ensure equal representation for women, in large part on the ground that without such representation, important points of view will be absent. There is much to be said about this large topic. But to anchor the discussion, I now turn to two more particular issues, both of considerable contemporary concern: diversity on the federal judiciary and affirmative action in higher education.

Judges

Are judges subject to conformity effects? Are they likely to cascade? Do like-minded judges move to extremes? What is the effect of anticipated and actual dissents? To answer these questions, I am going to go in some detail. My hope is that the discussion will be useful not only to lawyers and judges but also to all those interested in conformity in areas where independent judgments might be expected.

For an introduction to the problem, consider an important early study of judicial behavior on the influential District of Columbia Circuit.[29] The study found that a panel of three Republican-appointed judges is far more likely to strike down decisions of federal agencies (such as the Environmental Protection Agency) at the behest of industry than is a panel of two Republican appointees and one Democratic appointee. At first glance, that is odd. After all, two Republican appointees have a majority. Why is a panel with two Republican appointees so much less likely to strike down a federal agency decision than a panel with three Republican appointees?

At the individual level, the same study finds that group influences play a large role. I will get to some details before long, but here is vivid evidence: when sitting with two Republican appointees, a Democratic appointee is more likely to vote to strike down agency action, at the behest of industry, than is a Republican appointee when sitting with two Democratic appointees. For present purposes, it does not much matter whether the judge of a single party is actually persuaded or instead decides that it is simply not worthwhile to dissent publicly. In either case, the vote reflects social influences, in a process that is not entirely different from what is observed in the Asch experiments. What I am sketching goes by the name of "panel effects." It suggests that a judge's vote, in ideologically controversial cases, is greatly influenced by the other two judges on the panel.

Several studies over various periods of time find a strong tendency toward more extreme results when a panel consists of three judges from a single political party.[30] In brief, a panel of three Republican appointees shows extremely conservative voting patterns, and a panel of three Democratic appointees shows extremely liberal voting patterns. A background finding from an early study is that when industry challenges an environmental regulation, there is an extraordinary difference between the behavior of a Republican-appointed majority and that of a Democratic-appointed majority. In the relevant period, Republican-appointed majorities reversed agencies more than 50 percent of the time; Democratic-appointed majorities did so less than 15 percent of the time.[31] There are also significant findings of panel effects. Judges' votes are greatly affected by whether there is another judge, on that panel, appointed by a president from the same political party. Republican appointees are much more likely to accept an industry challenge if there is at least one Republican-appointed colleague on the panel. Democratic appointees are far less likely to accept such a challenge if there is at least one other Democratic appointee on the panel.[32] A single Democratic appointee, accompanied by two Republican appointees, was found to vote in favor of industry challenges more than 40 percent of the time, but when joined by one or more Democratic appointees, the Democratic appointee voted in favor of such challenges less than 30 percent of the time.[33]

By contrast, a single Republican appointee, sitting with two Democratic appointees, voted in favor of industry challenges less than 20 percent of the time.[34] Remarkably, a single Republican appointee, when accompanied by two Democratic appointees, was less likely to accept an industry challenge than a single Democratic appointee, when accompanied by two Republican appointees.

This study was undertaken a number of years ago, but other studies, and more recent ones, find the same basic patterns in many areas of the law.[35] It is reasonable to think that in ideologically contested areas, the political affiliation of the president who appointed a judge is a pretty good predictor of how that judge will vote. That is true. But often, a better predictor of how a judge will vote is *the political affiliation of the president who appointed the other two judges on the panel*. The simplest finding is that a Democratic appointee is fairly likely to vote in a stereotypically conservative direction when accompanied by two Republican appointees—in cases that involve sex discrimination, race discrimination, environmental protection, and much more. When a Democratic appointee sits with one Republican appointee and one Democratic appointee rather than with two Republican appointees, the likelihood of a stereotypically liberal vote increases significantly. When a Democratic appointee sits with two Democratic appointees, the likelihood of a stereotypically liberal vote skyrockets. Republican appointees show exactly the same pattern—in reverse.

This is a real testimony to the strength of social influences. In many areas of the law, a Democratic appointee, sitting with two Republican appointees, votes like a Republican appointee, whereas a Republican appointee, sitting with two Democratic appointees, votes like a Democratic appointee. How a Democratic appointee votes and how a Republican appointee votes are very much a function of whether they are accompanied by one or two people from their own party or none at all. For this reason, there is no single way, independent of group influences, that either a Republican or a Democratic appointee tends to vote—at least in ideologically contested areas of the law.

In a testimonial to group polarization, a panel of three Republican appointees is far more likely than a panel of two Republican appointees and one Democratic appointee to reverse an environmental decision when industry challenges that decision.[36] In one period (1995 to 2002), 71 percent of Republican appointees, on all-Republican panels, voted to accept industry challenges.[37] By contrast, 45 percent of Republican appointees, on two-to-one Republican panels, voted to accept such challenges—and 37.5 percent of Republican appointees so voted on two-to-one Democratic panels.[38] In an earlier period (1986–1994), the corresponding numbers were 80 percent, 48 percent, and 14 percent.[39] In a still earlier period (1970–1982), 100 percent of Republican appointees' votes, on all-Republican panels, were in favor of industry challenges. By contrast, only 45 percent of Republican appointees' votes, on two-to-one Republican panels, were in favor of industry challenges—and only 26 percent of Republican appointees' votes, on Democratic-majority panels, were in favor of such challenges.[40]

Aggregating this data, we can produce a broadly representative and nearly complete account of votes, within the D.C. Circuit, in environmental cases in the period between 1979 and 2002. (More recent court of appeals data, in other areas of the law, continue to show broadly similar patterns.) A simple calculation shows that in all-Republican panels, Republican appointees voted to accept industry challenges 80 percent of the time; that in two-to-one Republican panels, Republican appointees voted to accept such challenges 48 percent of the time; and that in two-to-one Democratic panels, Republican appointees voted to accept industry challenges only 27.5 of the time. And social influences of this kind are hardly limited to Republican appointees; they can be found among Democratic appointees as well. When an environmental group is challenging agency action, a panel of three Democratic appointees is more likely to accept the challenge than a panel of two Democratic appointees and one Republican appointee.[41] The likelihood that a Democratic appointee will vote in favor of an environmentalist challenge is highest when three Democratic appointees are on the panel—and lowest when the panel has two Republican appointees.[42]

A third study is more complicated.[43] Under the Supreme Court's decision in *Chevron v. NRDC*,[44] courts are supposed to uphold agency interpretations of law so long as the interpretations are "reasonable." But when do courts actually uphold such interpretations? The doctrine allows judges some room to maneuver, so that courts that are inclined to invalidate agency action might be able to find a plausible basis for doing so. An important question is when they will claim to have found that plausible basis. The relevant study strongly suggests that group influences play a role and that the potential for a dissent from a Democratic appointee is a strong deterrent to Republican appointees who are inclined to invalidate agency action.

For background, note that the study finds an exceedingly strong influence, within the court of appeals for the influential D.C. Circuit, of party affiliation on outcomes. If observers were to code cases very crudely, by taking account of whether industry or a public interest group is bringing the challenge, they would find that a majority of Republican appointees reach a conservative judgment 54 percent of the time, whereas a majority of Democratic appointees reach such a judgment merely 32 percent of the time.[45]

For present purposes, the most important finding is that there is a dramatic difference between politically diverse panels, with judges appointed by presidents of more than one party, and politically unified panels, with judges appointed by presidents of only one party. On divided panels in which a Republican-appointed majority of the court might be expected, on broadly speaking political grounds, to be hostile to the agency, the court nonetheless deferred to the agency 62 percent of the time. But on unified panels in which an all-Republican panel might be expected to be hostile to the agency, the court upheld the agency's interpretation only 33 percent of the time. Note that this was the only such finding in the data. When Democratic-appointed majority courts were expected to uphold the agency's decision on political grounds, they did so more than 70 percent of the time, whether unified (71 percent of the time) or divided (86 percent of the time). Consider the results in tabular form:[46]

	3–0 Republican panel	2–1 Republican panel	3–0 Democratic panel	2–1 Democratic panel
Uphold agency action	33%	62%	71%	86%
Invalidate agency action	67%	38%	29%	14%

It seems reasonable to speculate that the seemingly bizarre result—a 67 percent invalidation rate when Republican appointees are unified—reflects group influences and in particular group polarization. A group of all-Republican appointees might well take the relatively unusual step of rejecting an agency's interpretation, whereas a divided panel, with a built-in check on any tendency toward the unusual or extreme outcome, is more likely to take the conventional route. A likely reason is that the single Democratic appointee acts as a "whistleblower," discouraging the other judges from making a decision that is in tension with the Supreme Court's command to uphold agency interpretations of ambiguous statutes.[47]

Other factors are probably involved. When a court consists of a panel of judges with the same basic orientation, the median view, before deliberation begins, will be significantly different from what it would be with a panel of diverse judges. The argument pool will be very different as well. For example, a panel of three Republican appointees, tentatively inclined to invalidate the action of the Environmental Protection Agency (EPA), may offer a range of arguments in support of invalidation and relatively few in the other direction—even if the law, properly interpreted, favors validation. If the panel contains a judge who is inclined to uphold the EPA, the arguments that favor validation are far more likely to emerge and be pressed. Indeed, the very fact that the judge is a Democratic appointee increases the likelihood that this will occur, if that judge does not think of himself or herself as being part of the same "group" as the other panel members. (Recall that when people are connected by ties of solidarity, disagreement is much less likely.) And because corroboration of opinion leads to greater confidence and hence extremity, it is not surprising that a panel of three like-minded judges would lead to unusual and extreme results.

In this context, the effect is fortified by the possibility that the sole judge, being outnumbered on a three-judge panel, might produce a dissenting opinion in public. To be sure,

Supreme Court review is rare, and in the general run of cases, the prospect of such review probably does not have much of a deterrent effect on courts of appeals. But judges who write majority opinions are usually not enthusiastic about having to see and respond to dissenting opinions. And if the law actually favors the dissenting view, two judges, even if they would like to reverse the Environmental Protection Agency, might be influenced to adopt the easier course of validation. The evidence so suggests.[48]

A glance at the table above offers some countervailing data: A panel of three Democratic appointees is not more likely than a panel with two Democratic appointees to uphold agency action in cases in which Democratic appointees might be expected to want to uphold the agency. And in the context of a challenge from an environmental group, Republican appointees are not likely to vote differently if they are accompanied by two Democratic appointees, one Republican appointee, or two Republican appointees.[49] But in many important domains, at least, a panel of three like-minded judges does indeed behave differently from a panel with two.[50]

At this point a skeptic might note that lawyers make adversarial presentations before three-judge panels. Such a skeptic might insist that the size of the "argument pool" is determined by those presentations, not only and not even mostly by what members of the panel are inclined to say and to do. And undoubtedly the inclinations of judges are shaped, much of the time, by the contributions of advocates. But even if this is so, what matters, for purposes of the outcomes, are the inclinations of judges, whatever they are based on; and it is here that the existence of a single dissenter can make all the difference. In the punitive damage study discussed above, mock juries were presented with arguments from both sides, and polarization followed this presentation, as it has elsewhere. Notice in this regard that for the polarization hypothesis to hold, it is not necessary to know whether judges spend a great deal of time offering reasons to one another. Mere exposure to a conclusion is enough.[51] A system of simple votes, unaccompanied by reasons, should incline judges to polarize. Of course reasons, if they are good ones, are likely to make those votes especially persuasive.

It remains to investigate the normative issues. If likeminded judges go to extremes, should we be troubled? Is it good if a large effect is found from a single judge from a different party? More generally, is there reason to attempt to ensure diversity on the federal courts? To promote a degree of diversity on panels? Some people think that judges appointed by presidents of different political parties are not fundamentally different and that once on the bench, judges frequently surprise those who nominated them. The view is not entirely baseless, but it is misleading. Some appointees do disappoint the presidents who nominated them, but the availability heuristic should not fool us into thinking that these examples are typical. Judges appointed by Republican presidents are quite different from judges appointed by Democratic presidents. "Partisanship clearly affects how appellate courts review agency discretion."[52]

But it seems difficult to evaluate the underlying issues without taking a stand on the merits—without knowing what we want judges to do. Suppose that three Republican appointees are especially likely to uphold criminal convictions and that three Democratic appointees are especially likely to reverse those convictions. At first glance, one or the other is troubling only if we know whether we approve of one or another set of results. In the punitive damage study discussed above, the movement toward increased awards might be something to celebrate, not to deplore, if we conclude that the median of predeliberation awards is too low and that the increase, produced by group discussion, ensures more sensible awards. And if a view about what judges should do is the only possible basis for evaluation, we might conclude that those who prefer judges of a particular party should seek judges of that party and that group influences are essentially beside the point.

But the conclusion is too strong. In some cases, the law, properly interpreted, really does argue strongly for one or another view. The existence of diversity on a panel is likely to bring that fact to light and perhaps to move the panel's decision in the direction of what the law requires. The existence of politically diverse judges, and of a potential dissent, increases the probability that the law will be followed. The *Chevron* study, referred to above, strongly supports this point. The presence of a potential dissenter—in the form of a judge appointed by a president from another political party—creates a possible whistleblower who can reduce the likelihood of an incorrect or lawless decision. Through an appreciation of the nature of group influences, we can see the wisdom in an old idea: a decision is more likely to be right, and less likely to be political in a pejorative sense, if it is supported by judges with different predilections.

There is a further point. Suppose that in many areas, it is not clear, in advance, whether the appointees of Democratic or Republican presidents are correct. Suppose that we are genuinely uncertain. If so, there is reason to favor a situation in which the legal system has both, simply on the ground that through that route, more (reasonable) opinions are likely to be heard. And if we are genuinely uncertain, there may be reason to favor a mix of views merely by virtue of its moderating effect.

Consider an analogy. Modern law and policy are often made by independent regulatory commissions, such as the Federal Trade Commission, the Securities and Exchange Commission, the National Labor Relations Board, and the Federal Communications Commission. Much of the time, such agencies act through adjudication. They function in the same fashion as federal courts. And under federal statutes, Congress has attempted to ensure that these agencies are not monopolized by either Democrats or Republicans. The law requires that no more than a bare majority of agency members may be from a single party.

An understanding of group influences helps explain this requirement. An independent agency that is all Democratic or all Republican might move toward an extreme position, indeed a position that is more extreme than that of the median Democrat or Republican and possibly more extreme than that of any agency official standing alone. A requirement of bipartisan membership can operate as a check against movements of this kind. Congress was apparently aware of this general point. Closely attuned to the policy-making functions of the relevant institutions, it was careful to provide a safeguard against extreme movements.

Why do we fail to create similar safeguards for courts? Part of the answer must lie in a belief that unlike heads of independent regulatory commissions, judges are not policy makers. Their duty is to follow the law, not to make policy. An attempt to ensure bipartisan composition would seem inconsistent with the commitment to this belief. But the evidence I have discussed shows that judges are policy makers of an important kind and that their political commitments very much influence their votes. I do not mean to embrace any particular policy proposal here. But in principle, there is good reason to attempt to ensure a mix of perspectives within courts of appeals.

Of course the idea of diversity, or of a mix of perspectives, is hardly self-defining. It would not be appropriate to say that the federal judges should include people who refuse to obey the Constitution, who refuse to exercise the power of judicial review, or who think the Constitution allows suppression of political dissent and racial segregation. Here as elsewhere, the domain of appropriate diversity is limited. What is necessary is reasonable diversity, or diversity of reasonable views, and not diversity as such. People can certainly disagree about what reasonable diversity entails in this context. All that I am suggesting here is that there is such a thing as reasonable diversity and that it is important to ensure that judges, no less than anyone else, are exposed to it, and not merely through the arguments of advocates.

These points cast fresh light on a much-disputed issue: the legitimate role of the Senate in giving "advice and consent" to presidential appointments to the federal judiciary. Above all, an understanding of social influences suggests that the Senate has a responsibility to exercise its constitutional authority in order to ensure a reasonable diversity of view. The Constitution's history fully contemplates an independent role for the Senate in the selection of Supreme Court justices.[53] That independent role certainly authorizes the Senate to consider the general approach, and likely pattern of votes, of potential judges. There can be no doubt that the president considers the general approach of his or her nominees; the Senate is entitled to do so as well. Under good conditions, these simultaneous powers would bring about a healthy form of checks and balances, permitting each branch to counter the other. Indeed, that system is part and parcel of social deliberation about the direction of the federal judiciary.

Why might this view be rejected? It could be argued that there is only one legitimate approach to constitutional or statutory interpretation—that, for example, some version of originalism or textualism is the only such approach and that anyone who rejects that view is unreasonable. For true believers, it is pointless to argue for diverse views. Diversity is not necessary, or even valuable, if we already know what should be done and if competing views would simply cloud the issue. (In a scientific dispute, it is not helpful to include those who believe the earth is flat.) Or it might be argued that a deferential role for the Senate, combined with natural political competition and cycles, will produce a sensible mix over time. I do not deny this possibility. My only suggestions are that a high degree of diversity on the federal judiciary is desirable, that the Senate is entitled to pursue diversity, and that without such diversity, judicial panels will inevitably go in unjustified directions.

Diversity and Affirmative Action in Higher Education

Countless educational institutions pursue the goal of diversity. Most of America's large private and public institutions seek a wide range of views, faculty members, and students. There are some prominent exceptions; some institutions pride themselves on a high degree of homogeneity. And here as elsewhere, the idea of diversity needs to be clarified. Colleges and universities do not make special efforts to include students who collect Taylor Swift memorabilia, hate America, smell bad, or have low SATs. Such institutions are committed to diversity, but only to a certain degree and of a certain kind. It remains possible to argue, as many do, that they give excessive attention to diversity of some kinds and insufficient attention to diversity of other kinds. The only point I am making here is that they tend to be committed to diversity of a recognizable sort.

Some people think that the pursuit of diversity is a big mistake, at least for colleges and universities. They believe that only one factor matters: merit. To be sure, the idea of merit could be defined in many different ways, but according to the view I am considering, it refers to academic potential, measured principally by reference to grades and scores on standardized tests. We could qualify that view by suggesting that if people have grown up poor, in challenging family circumstances, or with a disability, their academic potential might not be adequately measured by grades and test scores. Fair enough. But there is no question that many colleges and universities are promoting a variety of goals that the word "merit" does not capture.

For example, a preference for children of alumni is most easily defended in purely economic terms. If institutions admit such children ("legacies"), they might be more likely to get donations. If institutions seek geographical diversity, they will obtain a range of perspectives. If they seek musicians and athletes or students with unusual tastes and passions, they will have an interesting mix of people. Let us focus for the moment on the commitment to *cognitive* diversity—on having students who have different experiences, values, perspectives, and information.

There are many reasons for this commitment. One involves simple market pressures; a school that has different sorts of students is more likely to be able to attract good faculty members and good students. Of course people's preferences and values vary, and some people want to go to places that are relatively homogeneous. But this seems to be the exception rather than the rule. And there is another justification for diversity, one that has received considerable attention within courts[54] and that is closely related to my topic here. The idea is that education is likely to be better if the school has people with different views, perspectives, and experiences.

In principle, that idea need not focus on the question of race at all. If a university has students from New York, California, Ohio, Texas, Florida, Iowa, Mississippi, and Alabama, it is likely to have more cognitive diversity than if its students come only from New York. If an American university seeks cognitive diversity, it might well make special efforts to attract and admit students from other nations—China and France, Germany and Denmark, Japan and South Africa. Students at different ends of the income distribution are also likely to have different perspectives.

In some places, women are, as a class, stronger applicants than men. People can dispute whether a university might decide that it wants to have a sufficiently large percentage of men—say, at least 40 percent—even if that means it will be giving a preference to them. And of course there is a trade-off between cognitive diversity and other values. Pure academic potential may cut in one direction; the pursuit of diversity might cut in another.

It is important to see that a university can pursue cognitive diversity without discriminating against anyone on grounds that are generally agreed to be illicit. In 2018, it was alleged that some elite universities are discriminating against Asian Americans, using interviews, or other factors, to impose some kind of quota on their numbers. In the view of many people, using quotas is utterly unacceptable; it cannot be distinguished from similar ceilings on the number of Jews from decades before. Let us bracket the question whether the allegation is true. It is entirely possible to insist that universities may not discriminate against Asian Americans while also insisting that they can pursue diversity of various kinds, through geographic preferences, consideration of economic background, emphasis on extracurricular activities, and so forth. To be sure, some difficult questions might arise here about whether discrimination is being shrouded and about whether there really is a line between discrimination against one group and preferences for another.

Let us put those questions to one side and focus on the question of race-based affirmative action. In that context, an argument in favor of *cognitive* diversity was approved in Justice Lewis Powell's decisive opinion in the *Bakke* case,[55] an opinion that has the unusual distinction of having settled, for a period of decades, the constitutionality of affirmative action in higher education. My goal here is to offer a qualified defense of Justice Powell's view. I urge that in some educational settings, racial diversity is important for ensuring a broad array of experiences and ideas and that in those settings, narrowly tailored affirmative action programs should be constitutionally permissible.

Justice Powell insisted that a diverse student body is a constitutionally acceptable goal for higher education.[56] The central reason is that universities should be allowed to ensure a "robust exchange of ideas," an interest connected with the first amendment itself.[57] Justice Powell acknowledged that this interest seemed strongest in the context of undergraduate education, where views are formed on a large number of topics. But even in a medical school, "the contribution of diversity is substantial."[58] A medical student having a particular background, including a particular racial background, "may bring to a professional school of medicine experiences, outlooks, and ideas that enrich the training of its student body and better equip its graduates to render with understanding their vital service to humanity."[59] Justice Powell also emphasized that doctors "serve a heterogeneous population" and suggested that graduate admissions decisions are concerned with contributions that follow formal education.[60]

Thus Justice Powell concluded that the crucial question was whether a race-conscious admission program, giving benefits to people because they are members of racial minority groups, was a necessary means of promoting the legitimate goal of diversity. Here he reached his famous conclusion that racial or ethnic background could be a "plus" in the admissions decision, though quotas would not be allowed.[61] For Justice Powell, a legitimate admissions program should be "flexible enough to consider all pertinent elements of diversity in light of the particular qualifications of the applicant, and to place them on the same footing for consideration, although not necessarily according to them the same weight."[62] Thus it would be acceptable to promote "beneficial educational pluralism" by considering a range of factors, including "demonstrated compassion, a history of overcoming disadvantage, ability to communicate with the poor, or other qualifications deemed important."[63]

Justice Powell's arguments have carried the day, even decades later.[64] At least in education, the court has held that while racial quotas are unacceptable, race can be considered as a "plus," at least for the benefit of African American applicants. To be sure, some members of the court believe that the Constitution requires race neutrality, and it is possible that before long, the court will forbid race to be considered in any way. Should it?

My central concern here is the principal basis for Justice Powell's conclusion: the value of ensuring a "robust exchange of ideas" in the classroom and the legitimacy of promoting racial diversity in order to ensure that exchange. To understand the contemporary relevance of Justice Powell's opinion, it is necessary to outline the constitutional principles governing affirmative action programs. The court has settled on the view that affirmative action programs, like all other programs embodying racial discrimination, should be subject to "strict scrutiny" from courts and invalidated unless they are the least restrictive means of achieving a compelling state interest. It is also clear that past "societal discrimination," meaning discrimination in the nation's past, is not a legitimate basis for discrimination against whites.[65] At least for the moment, it is equally clear that narrow, remedial affirmative action programs are acceptable if they are specifically designed to correct for proven past discrimination by the institution that is acting affirmatively.[66]

What remains unclear is when, if ever, a public institution is permitted to justify affirmative action by reference to "forward-looking" justifications, not involving a remedy for past discrimination.[67] A state might, for example, try to defend affirmative action in hiring police by urging that a police force will simply be more effective if it contains African Americans among others—especially in a community that contains people of multiple races. Justice Powell was really offering a similar claim about higher education: whether or not a college or university has itself discriminated against African Americans or others, it should be permitted to discriminate in favor of them if it is doing so as a means of ensuring a "robust exchange of ideas." But the court offered a general pronouncement about forward-looking justifications.

As we have seen, there is no doubt that universities are permitted to promote diversity and dissent by seeking a mix of faculty members and students. They can seek people with different backgrounds, different talents, and different opinions. Efforts of this kind are pervasive; this is what many admissions offices try to do. True, some serious free speech issues might be raised if an admissions office discriminates in favor of, or against, particular points of view. But even if public institutions are barred from pursuing diversity of ideas by discriminating directly against some points of view, such institutions are surely permitted, without offending the first amendment, to seek a variety of backgrounds and experiences in the hope that better discussions will result.

To be sure, race is different, and if an institution discriminates against people because of their skin color, it faces a heavy burden of justification, even if the people against whom it discriminates are white. But if Justice Powell is right, affirmative action programs can be similarly justified. The simple idea here is that racially diverse populations are likely to increase the range of thoughts and perspectives and to reduce the risks of conformity, cascades, and polarization associated with group influences. We have seen that on the judiciary, judges with diverse views can act as "whistleblow-ers," correcting ill-considered views of the law. In educational institutions, a high degree of diversity, including racial diver-sity, might have the same effect. On some issues, a racially uniform class might polarize to an unjustified position, sim-ply because students do not hear important perspectives.

For example, we can easily imagine all-white classrooms discussing the issue of racial profiling; the absence of racial diversity could be a serious problem. Those who have not had bad experiences, as a result of such profiling, will lack crucial information. Justice Sandra Day O'Connor offered these comments on African American justice Thurgood Marshall: "Justice Marshall brought a special perspective. . . . His was the mouth of a man who knew the anguish of the silenced and gave them a voice. . . . I have been perhaps most personally affected by Justice Marshall as a raconteur. . . . Oc-casionally, at Conference meetings, I still catch myself look-ing expectantly for his raised brow and his twinkling eye, hoping to hear, just once more, another story that would, by and by, perhaps change the way I see the world."[68]

What was true for Justice O'Connor is true for white stu-dents in many educational settings. In the context of racial profiling, and in many other imaginable cases, a degree of racial diversity is likely to introduce valuable information and perspectives. These may change how the group sees the world, whether or not it leads to a different conclusion on the merits.

To say this is not to make the absurd claim that white people all agree with one another about racial profiling or that African Americans have the same experiences and opinions about that complex issue. And in light of the fact that members of all races contain people with a range of both favorable and unfavorable views about racial profiling, it would be possible to respond that any problem, if it exists, is not because the group is all white but if and because its members begin with a uniform view of racial profiling. What matters is diversity of ideas, not racial diversity. And if this is so, what, if anything, is added by promoting diversity not of views but of racial background?

The answer must be that African Americans, by virtue of their experience, are able to add something to the discussion as such. That seems far from implausible. If students need to know something about the magnitude and the experience of racial profiling, those who have been subject to such profiling will be able to offer novel insights. And if African Americans do, in fact, have an unusually high degree of hostility to racial profiling, that is by itself a point worthwhile to know and try to understand. So too if they do not show such hostility. Of course supplemental readings could be used to expose people to diverse views. The value of diversity lies not simply in learning about facts but also in *seeing* a range of perspectives, including the emotions attached to them—and in being in the actual physical presence of those who have those perspectives and perhaps cannot be easily dismissed.

These points might be used by a fair-minded institution to defend a set of policies designed to ensure a reasonable diversity of view in classroom discussions. Because of the importance of a wide range of ideas to the educational enterprise, the goal seems both legitimate and compelling. Are affirmative action programs the least restrictive means of promoting that goal? The answer depends on the nature of those programs. It is easy to imagine cautious efforts, using race as a factor, in which the "least restrictive means" test is indeed satisfied. And that point is sufficient to suggest that Justice Powell's approach is essentially correct.

To be sure, the same arguments about the importance of diverse views might be enlisted very broadly and in circumstances that might seem less attractive. Imagine, for example, an effort by a mostly African American university to point to the need for diversity as a way of defending discrimination against African Americans and in favor of whites. Such a university might claim that it wants significant representation by whites in order to reduce the risks from group influences and to improve the quality of discussion. It does indeed follow, from what I have said thus far, that this argument is legitimate. A classroom that is entirely African American might well suffer from conformity effects and polarization, and an educational institution might want to correct the situation.

If courts should be suspicious of the argument in this context, it is because they do not trust the sincerity of those who make it. Courts might believe that the reference to diversity is actually a pretext for an illicit discriminatory motive. But it is easy to imagine cases in which diversity is the real concern and no pretext is involved. The argument I am making is narrow and modest. In some cases, racial diversity is important for improving the educational process within the relevant school. But in some cases, the claim seems extremely weak. Would a mathematics class, or a course in physics, be improved if it contained a degree of racial diversity? This seems unlikely. If courts are going to scrutinize affirmative action programs, they should not offer a blanket ruling for or against a diversity rationale in higher education. They should accept that rationale in the context of undergraduate education, but not for programs for which racial diversity is not necessary to promote a "robust exchange of ideas." In the context of law school, the centrality of racial issues to important aspects of legal education should be enough to allow narrowly tailored affirmative action programs to survive constitutional scrutiny.

Conclusion

Conformity and Its Discontents

Human beings pay close attention to the informational and reputational signals sent by others. These signals produce conformity, even in cases in which many people have reason to believe, on the basis of their private information, that others are mistaken or worse. Informational and reputational influences also produce cascades, in which people do not rely on, and fail to disclose, the information they themselves have. Cascades and errors occur spontaneously when people take account of the decisions and statements of their predecessors. Errors are magnified when people are rewarded for conformity—and minimized when people are rewarded not for correct individual decisions but for correct decisions at the group level.

Cascades, like conformity, are not a problem in themselves. Sometimes cascades produce good outcomes, at least compared to a situation in which people rely solely on their own information. The real problem is that when cascades are occurring, people do not disclose information from which others would benefit. The result is that both individuals and private and public groups can blunder, sometimes catastrophically. Institutions involved in making, enforcing, and interpreting the law are subject to conformity and cascade effects. Government has often blundered as a result. We have seen that within courts, precedential cascades are highly likely, especially in complex areas; and in such areas, cascades tend to be both self-perpetuating and self-insulating.

The general lesson is clear. It is extremely important to devise institutions that promote disclosure of private views and private information. Institutions that instead reward conformity are prone to failure; institutions are far more likely to prosper if they create a norm of openness and dissent. The point very much bears on the risks of group polarization. Groups of like-minded people are likely to go to extremes, simply because of limited argument pools and reputational considerations. The danger is that the resulting movements in opinion will be unjustified. It is extremely important to create "circuit breakers" and to devise institutional arrangements that will serve to counteract movements that could not be supported if people had a wider range of information.

These points have implications for numerous issues in law and policy. I have focused on a small subset of those issues here. We have seen that an appreciation of social influences casts new light on the expressive function of law. Simply by virtue of what it says, and even if it is rarely enforced, law can affect the behavior of those who are unsure whether to engage in certain conduct—and also the behavior of those who are unsure whether to challenge those who engage in that conduct. Bans on smoking in public and on sexual harassment are cases in point. Law's effectiveness, in this regard, lies in its power to give a signal about appropriate behavior, and also to dissipate pluralistic ignorance, by providing information about what other people think is appropriate behavior. A legal enactment can operate in the same fashion as Solomon Asch's confederates and Stanley Milgram's experimenter. Because people care about the reactions of others, law's expressive function will be heightened if the relevant conduct is visible; bans on smoking in public places are an obvious example.

For the same reason, that function will be weakened if prospective lawbreakers live in a supportive subcommunity; consider bans on the use of narcotics. With an understanding of social influences, we can therefore make some predictions about when law is likely to be effective merely by virtue of what it says—and about when law will be ineffective unless it is accompanied by vigorous enforcement activity.

I have suggested that many of the institutions in the U.S. Constitution serve to reduce the likelihood of bad consequences from conformity, cascades, and group polarization. Such institutions increase the likelihood that important information, and alternative points of view, will receive a public airing. The system of bicameralism is the most obvious example, producing a system in which lawmaking is done by two institutions with different cultures, thus creating a potential check on unjustified movements. I have also urged that the framers' most distinctive contribution consisted not in their endorsement of deliberative democracy, which was uncontroversial, but in their commitment to heterogeneity in government, seeing (in Alexander Hamilton's words) the "jarring of parties" as a method for "promoting deliberation."

More controversially, I have suggested that an understanding of social influences suggests the importance of ensuring a high degree of diversity on the federal bench. It is foolish to pretend that Republican appointees do not, as a class, differ from Democratic appointees; and we have reason to appreciate the value, on any panel, of having a potential "whistleblower," in the form of one judge of a different party from the other two. Of course judges are rarely lawless, but a group of like-minded judges is prone to go to extremes. An appreciation of social influences on belief and behavior also supports the legitimacy of efforts to promote racial diversity in higher education, at least where such diversity is likely to improve learning.

Even if occasionally alarming, much of the behavior discussed here attests to the reasonableness and good sense of ordinary people. In the face of doubt, we do well to pay attention to the views of others. After all, they might know better than we do. It is prudent to be cautious about challenging other people, not only because they might be right but also because people do not always like to be challenged. Even in the most freedom-loving societies, people dissent at their peril. A reluctance to disagree is not merely prudent; it is often courteous too. But conformity creates severe dangers. Behavior that is sensible, prudent, and courteous is likely to lead individuals and societies to blunder, simply because people fail to learn about facts or opinions from which they would benefit.

It is usual to think that those who conform are serving the general interest and that dissenters are antisocial, even selfish.

In a way this is true. In some settings, conformists strengthen social bonds, whereas dissenters imperil them or at least introduce tension. But in an important respect, the usual thought has things backward. Much of the time, it is in the interest of the individual to follow the crowd but in the social interest for individuals to say and do what they think best. Well-functioning institutions take steps to discourage conformity and to promote dissent, partly to protect the rights of dissenters but mostly to protect interests of their own.

NOTES

PREFACE

1   Anna Collar provides a valuable discussion in *Religious Networks in the Roman Empire* (2014).

2   The classic treatment, emphasizing game theory and complementary to some of the discussion here, is Edna Ullmann-Margalit, *The Emergence of Norms* (1976).

3   Whitney v. California, 274 US 357, 376 (1927) (Brandeis, J., concurring).

4   Bob Dylan, "Absolutely Sweet Marie" (1966), at https://www.bob dylan.com.

INTRODUCTION. THE POWER OF SOCIAL INFLUENCES

1   *See* David Schkade et al., *What Happened on Deliberation Day?* 95 Calif. L. Rev. 915 (2007).

2   *See* David Schkade, Cass R. Sunstein, and Daniel Kahneman, *Deliberating about Dollars: The Severity Shift*, 100 Colum. L. Rev. 1139 (2001).

3   The statements in this paragraph are based principally on William Landes et al., *Rational Judicial Behavior: A Statistical Study*, 1 J. Legal Analysis 775 (2009); Cass R. Sunstein et al., *Are Judges Political?* (2006); and Richard L. Revesz, *Environmental Regulation, Ideology, and the DC Circuit*, 83 Va. L. Rev. 1717, 1755 (1997). To the same general effect, *see* Frank Cross and Emerson Tiller, *Judicial Partisanship and Obedience to Legal Doctrine*, 107 Yale L.J. 2155 (1998). Cross and Tiller found that a panel of three Republican judges is far more likely to reject agency action, thus reaching a conclusion predicted of that panel on political grounds, than is a panel of two Republicans and one Democrat. The literature on panel effects is voluminous and offers a number of qualifications

and refinements. A valuable discussion, with data, is Pauline Kim, *Deliberation and Strategy on the United States Courts of Appeals: An Empirical Exploration of Panel Effects*, 157 U. Pa. L. Rev. 1319 (2009). Also valuable, with an overview and analysis of multiple studies, is Joshua Fischman, *Interpreting Circuit Court Voting Patterns: A Social Interactions Framework*, 31 J. Law, Economics, and Organization 808 (2015). Christina Boyd et al., *Untangling the Causal Effects of Sex on Judging*, 54 Am. J. Polit. Sci. 389 (2010), explores whether the presence of a female judge has an effect on how male judges vote—and finds that in sex discrimination cases, it does have an effect (increasing by 10 percent the likelihood that a judge decides in favor of a party alleging sex discrimination). Morgan Hazelton et al., *Panel Effects in Administrative Law: A Study of Rules, Standards, and Judicial Whistleblowing*, 71 S.M.U. L. Rev. 445 (2018), explores whether different areas of administrative law show more panel effects. Jonathan Kastellec, *Panel Composition and Voting on the U.S. Courts of Appeals over Time*, 64 Polit. Res. Q. 377 (2011), finds that panel composition has had an effect on judicial behavior only in relatively recent years. Lewis Wasserman and John Connolly, *Unipolar Panel Effects and Ideological Commitment*, 31 A.B.A. J. Lab. & Emp. Law 537 (2016), finds that in certain free speech cases, Democratic appointees are unaffected by panel composition, but Republican appointees are significantly affected.

4 *See* Luther Gulick, *Administrative Reflections from World War II* (1948).

5 *See* Harold H. Gardner, Nathan L. Kleinman, and Richard J. Butler, *Workers' Compensation and Family and Medical Leave Act Claim Contagion*, 20 J. Risk and Uncertainty 89, 101–10 (2000).

6 *See*, for example, George A. Akerlof, Janet L. Yellen, and Michael L. Katz, *An Analysis of Out-of-Wedlock Childbearing in the United States*, 111 Q.J. Econ. 277 (1996).

7 *See* Edward Glaeser, E. Sacerdote, and Jose Scheinkman, *Crime and Social Interactions*, 111 Q.J. Econ. 507 (1996).

8 *See* Robert Kennedy, *Strategy Fads and Strategic Positioning: An Empirical Test for Herd Behavior in Prime-Time Television Programming*, 50 J. Industrial Econ. 57 (2002).

9 *See* Andrew F. Daughety and Jennifer F. Reinganum, *Stampede to Judgment*, 1 Am. L. & Econ. Rev. 158 (1999).

10 Hence Mill's claim that "the peculiar evil of silencing the expression of an opinion is, that it is robbing the human race; posterity as well as the existing generation; those who dissent from the opinion, still more than those who hold it. If the opinion is right, they are deprived of the opportunity of exchanging error for truth; if wrong, they lose, what is almost as great a benefit, the clearer perception and livelier impression of truth, produced by its collision with error." John Stuart Mill, *On Liberty*, in *Utilitarianism: On Liberty; Considerations on Representative Government* 85 (H. B. Acton ed. 1972).

11 *See* Alan B. Krueger, *What Makes a Terrorist?* (10th anniversary edition, 2018).

12 *See* Timur Kuran, *Ethnic Norms and Their Transformation through Reputational Cascades*, 27 J. Legal Stud. 623, 648 (1998).

13 *See* Cass R. Sunstein, *Why They Hate Us: The Role of Social Dynamics*, 25 Harv. J.L. & Pub. Pol'y 429 (2002).

14 *See* Russell Hardin, *The Crippled Epistemology of Extremism*, in *Political Rationality and Extremism* 3, 16 (Albert Breton et al. eds. 2002).

15 *See* Joseph Henrich et al., *Group Report: What Is the Role of Culture in Bounded Rationality?*, in *Bounded Rationality: The Adaptive Toolbox* 353–54 (Gerd Gigerenzer and Reinhard Selten eds. 2001), for an entertaining outline in connection with food choice decisions. For example, "Many Germans believe that drinking water after eating cherries is deadly; they also believe that putting ice in soft drinks is unhealthy. The English, however, rather enjoy a cold drink of water after some cherries; and Americans love icy refreshments." *Id.* at 353. *See also* Paul Omerod, *Butterfly Economics* (1993), for a popular account.

16 Mathew Adler, *Expressivist Theories of Law: A Skeptical Overview*, 148 U. Pa. L. Rev. 1363 (2000); *see also* Deborah Hellman, *Symposium: The Expressive Dimension of Governmental Action: Philosophical and Legal Perspectives*, 60 Md. L. Rev. 465 (2001).

17 *See* Robert Kagan and Jerome Skolnick, *Banning Smoking: Compliance without Enforcement*, in *Smoking Policy: Law, Politics, and Culture* 78 (Robert L. Rabin ed. 1999).

CHAPTER 1. HOW CONFORMITY WORKS

1 *See* Dominic Abrams et al., *Knowing What to Think by Knowing Who You Are: Self-Categorization and the Nature of Norm Formation, Conformity, and Group Polarization*, 29 British J. Soc. Psychol. 97 (1990). Group membership and self-categorization are emphasized in John Turner et al., *Rediscovering the Social Group: A Self-Categorization Theory* 42–67 (1987).

2 *See* Muzafer Sherif, *An Experimental Approach to the Study of Attitudes*, 1 Sociometry 90 (1937). A good outline can be found in Lee Ross and Richard Nisbet, *The Person and the Situation* 28–30 (1991).

3 *See* Ross and Nisbet, *supra* note 2, at 29.

4 *See id.*

5 *Id.*

6 *See id.* at 29–30.

7 Jonathan Thomas and Ruth McFadyen, *The Confidence Heuristic: A Game-Theoretic Approach*, 16 J. Econ. Psych. 97 (1995); Paul Price and Eric Stone, *Intuitive Evaluation of Likelihood Judgment Producers: Evidence for a Confidence Heuristic*, 17 J. Behav. Decision Making 39 (2004); Dan Bang et al., *Does Interaction Matter? Testing Whether a Confidence Heuristic Can Replace Interaction in Collective Decision-Making*, 26 Consciousness and Cognition 13 (2014).

8 *See* the discussion of authority in Robert Cialdini, *Influence: The Psychology of Persuasion* 208–36 (1993). For evidence that minority views can be influential if they are held by consistent, confident people, *see* Robert Bray et al., *Social Influence by Group Members with Minority Opinions*, 43 J. Personality and Soc. Psychol. 78 (1982).

9 *See* Abrams, *supra* note 1, at 99–104.

10 *See* the overview in Solomon Asch, *Opinions and Social Pressure*, in *Readings about the Social Animal* 13 (Elliott Aronson ed. 1995).

11 Solomon Asch, *Social Psychology* 453 (1952).

12 Asch, *Opinions and Social Pressure*, *supra* note 10, at 13.

13 *See id.* at 16.

14 *See id.*

15 *See* Rod Bond and Peter Smith, *Culture and Conformity: A Meta-Analysis of Studies Using Asch's Line Judgment Task*, 119 Psychol. Bulletin 111, 116 (1996).

16 *See id.* at 118.

17 *See id.* at 128.

18 *See* Ronald Friend et al., *A Puzzling Misinterpretation of the Asch "Conformity" Study*, 20 Eur. J. of Soc. Psychol. 29, 37 (1990). Also valuable is Richard Griggs et al., *The Disappearance of Independence in Textbook Coverage of Asch's Social Pressure Experiments*, 42 Teaching of Psych. 137 (2015).

19 Asch, *Social Psychology*, *supra* note 11, at 457–58.

20 *Id.* at 466.

21 *See id.* at 470.

22 *See id.*

23 It would be possible to question this explanation, however, on the ground that some of these conformists might have been embarrassed to admit they were vulnerable to peer influence, entirely apart from a belief that the peers might have been right.

24 *See* Robert Shiller, *Irrational Exuberance* 149–50 (2000).

25 *See* Bond and Smith, *supra* note 15, at 124.

26 *See* Asch, *Opinions and Social Pressure*, *supra* note 10, at 23–24.

27 *See* Robert Baron et al., *Group Process, Group Decision, Group Action* 66 (2d ed. 1999).

28 Asch, *Opinions and Social Pressure*, *supra* note 10, at 21.

29 *Id.*

30 *See* Sophie Sowden et al., *Quantifying Compliance and Acceptance through Public and Private Social Conformity, Consciousness and Cognition* 65 Conscious Cogn. 359 (2018).

31 *Id.*

32 B. Douglas Bernheim and Christine Exley, *Understanding Conformity: An Experimental Investigation* (2015), at https://www.hbs.edu.

33 *See* B. Douglas Bernheim, *A Theory of Conformity*, 102 J. Polit. Econ. 841 (1994).

34 Spee Kosloff et al., *Assessing Relationships between Conformity and Meta-Traits in an Asch-Like Paradigm*, 12 J. Influence 90 (2017).

35 *See* Kees Van Den Bos et al., *Reminders of Behavioral Disinhibition Increase Public Conformity in the Asch Paradigm and Behavioral Affiliation with Ingroup Members*, Front. Psych. (2015), at https://www.frontiersin.org.

36 John Stuart Mill, *On Liberty*, in *Utilitarianism: On Liberty; Considerations on Representative Government* 73 (H. B. Acton ed. 1972).

37 *See* Baron et al., *Group Process*, *supra* note 27.

38 *See id.*

39 *See* Robert Baron et al., *The Forgotten Variable in Conformity Research: Impact of Task Importance on Social Influence*, 71 J. Personality and Social Psychol. 915 (1996).

40 *See id.* at 923.

41 *See id.*

42 *See* Daniel Goldstein et al., *Why and When Do Simple Heuristics Work?*, in *Bounded Rationality: The Adaptive Toolbox* 174 (Gerd Gigerenzer and Reinhard Selten eds. 2001).

43 *See id.*

44 Baron et al., *Forgotten Variable*, *supra* note 39, at 925.

45 *Id.*

46 *See* Asch, *Opinions and Social Pressure*, *supra* note 10.

47 *See* Baron et al., *Group Process*, *supra* note 27, at 119–20.

48 *See id.* at 18. The finding here is reminiscent of the tale of "The Emperor's New Clothes," in which a single voice of sanity was necessary and sufficient to expose the truth. *See* Hans Christian Anderson, *The Emperor's New Suit*, in *Shorter Tales* (Jean Hersholt trans. 1948; originally published 1837).

49 *See* Brooke Harrington, *Pop Finance: Investor Clubs and New Investor Populism* (2008).

50 *See id.*

51 *See* Abrams et al., *supra* note 1, at 104–10.

52 *See* Baron et al., *Group Process*, *supra* note 27, at 66. The point is stressed at various places in Turner, *supra* note 1; *see*, for example, pp. 151–70.

53 *See* Abrams et al., *supra* note 1, at 106–8.

54 *See id.*

55 *See id.* at 108. By contrast, people who thought they were members of a different group actually gave more accurate, nonconforming answers when speaking publicly, which creates an interesting puzzle: why was there more accuracy in public than in private statements? The puzzle is solved if we consider the likelihood that

subjects could consider it an affirmative good to disagree with people from another group (even if they secretly suspected that those people might be right). In the real world, this effect may be heightened when people are asked whether they agree with opponents or antagonists; they might say no even when the answer is yes, simply because agreement carries costs, either to reputation or to self-conception.

There is a noteworthy finding about the nature of minority influences: they have a larger impact on people's privately expressed views than on their publicly expressed views. *See* Baron et al., *Group Process*, *supra* note 27, at 79–80. For example, minority members who express enthusiasm for gay rights, or opposition to gay rights, affect anonymous opinions more than publicly stated opinions. *See id.* at 80. This point has obvious implications for the effects of secret votes and ballots.

56 Consider the fact that the least conformity, and the greatest accuracy, was found when people who thought of themselves in a different group were speaking publicly. At the same time, the largest number of conforming, inaccurate responses came when people thought of themselves in the same group and were speaking publicly—even though the number of inaccurate *private* responses in that experimental condition was not notably higher than in other conditions. *See* Abrams et al., *supra* note 1, at 108.

57 There are other noteworthy findings about the Asch experiments. For example, cultures that are traditionally described as collectivist show greater conformity effects than cultures that are traditionally described as individualist. "On the basis of our discussion, we would expect differences in susceptibility to social influence between individualist and collectivist cultures to be even greater when the task was, for example, an opinion issue." Bond and Smith, *supra* note 15, at 128. Since the 1950s, there has been a linear reduction in conformity, suggesting that over time people have become more willing to reject the views of the majority. *See id.* at 129. Women are more likely to conform than men. *See id.* at 130. The latter finding is worth emphasizing; it fits well with the general finding that members of low-status groups are less likely to speak out within heterogeneous organizations. *See* Caryn Christenson and Ann

Abbott, *Team Medical Decision Making*, in *Decision Making in Health Care* 267, 273–76 (Gretchen Chapman and Frank Sonnenberg eds. 2000). This last point suggests the importance of creating mechanisms to ensure that low-status people speak and are heard.

58 This unconventional interpretation is set out in Thomas Blass, *The Milgram Paradigm after 35 Years: Some Things We Now Know about Obedience to Authority*, in *Obedience to Authority: Critical Perspectives on the Milgram Paradigm* 35, 38–44 (Thomas Blass ed. 1999). *See also* Shiller, *supra* note 24, at 150–51. Milgram's experiments remain highly controversial, and the issue of how to interpret them continues to provoke discussion. Mel Slater et al., *A Virtual Reprise of the Stanley Milgram Obedience Experiments*, 4 PLoS ONE 1 (2006), studies the obedience experiments in a virtual setting; it finds that subjects responded as if the situation were real and also finds responses compatible with those in Milgram's experiments. S. Alexander Haslam and Stephen Reicher, *Contesting the "Nature" of Conformity: What Milgram and Zimbardo's Studies Really Show*, 10 PLoS Biology 1 (2012), emphasizes the subjects' identification with the experimenter and a corresponding belief that the experimenter is likely to be right—an explanation that fits with what I offer in the text. Gina Perry, *Behind the Shock Machine: The Untold Story of the Notorious Milgram Psychology Experiments* (2013) is too provocative (I think), but it has some useful details and can be read to fit with the Asch-like explanation that Blass offers and on which I rely here. An alternative perspective, worth careful attention, suggests that Milgram's studies should be seen "not as demonstrations of conformity or obedience, but as explorations of the power of social identity–based leadership to induce active and committed followership." *See* Stephen Reicher et al., *Working toward the Experimenter: Reconceptualizing Obedience within the Milgram Framework as Obedience-Based Followership*, 7 Perspectives on Psychological Sci. 315 (2012).

59 *See* Stanley Milgram, *Behavioral Study of Obedience*, in *Readings about the Social Animal* 23 (7th ed. 1995).

60 *Id.* at 24.

61 *See id.* at 25.

62 *Id.* at 27.

63 *Id.* at 29.

64 *Id.* at 30.

65 *See* Stanley Milgram, *Obedience to Authority* 35 (1974).

66 *See id.* at 23.

67 *Id.* at 55.

68 *See id.* at 55–57.

69 *See id.* at 58.

70 Jerry Burger, *Replicating Milgram: Would People Still Obey Today?*, 64 Am. Psych. 1 (2009).

71 *See id.* at 34.

72 *See* Blass, *supra* note 58, at 42–44.

73 *See* Milgram, *Obedience to Authority*, *supra* note 65, at 113–22.

74 *See id.* at 119.

75 *See id.* at 118.

76 *See id.*

CHAPTER 2. CASCADES

1 *See* Matthew J. Salganik, Peter Sheridan Dodds, and Duncan J. Watts, *Experimental Study of Inequality and Unpredictability in an Artificial Cultural Market*, 311 Science 854 (2006); *see also* Matthew Salganik and Duncan Watts, *Leading the Herd Astray: An Experimental Study of Self-Fulfilling Prophecies in an Artificial Cultural Market*, 71 Soc. Psychol. Q. 338 (2008); and Matthew Salganik and Duncan Watts, *Web-Based Experiments for the Study of Collective Social Dynamics in Cultural Markets*, 1 Topics in Cognitive Sci. 429 (2009).

2 Salganik and Watts, *Leading the Herd Astray*, *supra* note 1.

3 *See* Timur Kuran and Cass R. Sunstein, *Availability Cascades and Risk Regulation*, 51 Stan. L. Rev. 683, 703–5 (1999).

4 *See* Andrew F. Daughety and Jennifer F. Reinganum, *Stampede to Judgment*, 1 Am. L. & Econ. Rev. 158 (1999).

5 I draw here on David Hirshleifer, *The Blind Leading the Blind*, in *The New Economics of Human Behavior* 188, 193–94 (Marianno Tommasi and Kathryn Ierulli eds. 1995).

6 *Id.* at 195. For valuable treatments, with an emphasis on people's failure to see the extent to which their predecessors simply followed others, *see* Erik Eyster and Matthew Rabin, *Naïve Herding in Rich-Information Settings*, 2 Am. Econ. J.: Microecon. 221 (2010); and

Erik Eyster and Matthew Rabin, *Extensive Imitation Is Harmful and Irrational*, 129 Q.J. Econ. 1861 (2014).

7   *See* Gina Kolata, *Risk of Breast Cancer Halts Hormone Replacement Study*, New York Times, at www.nytimes.com (July 11, 2002).

8   Hirshleifer, *supra* note 5, at 204.

9   John F. Burnum, *Medical Practice a la Mode*, 317 New Eng. J. Med. 1201, 1220 (1987).

10 *See* Sushil Bikhchandani et al., *Learning from the Behavior of Others: Conformity, Fads, and Informational Cascades*, 12 J. Econ. Persp. 151, 167 (1998).

11 *See* Tim O'Shea, *The Creation of a Market: How Did the Whole HRT Thing Get Started in the First Place?*, Mercola, at www.mercola.com (July 2001).

12 *See* Eric Talley, *Precedential Cascades: An Appraisal*, 73 So. Cal. L. Rev. 87 (1999).

13 *See* Daughety and Reinganum, *supra* note 4, at 161–65.

14 *See* Lisa Anderson and Charles Holt, *Information Cascades in the Laboratory*, 87 Am. Econ. Rev. 847 (1997).

15 *See* Angela Hung and Charles Plott, *Information Cascades: Replication and an Extension to Majority Rule and Conformity-Rewarding Institutions*, 91 Am. Econ. Rev. 1508, 1515 (2001).

16 Thus 72 percent of subjects followed Bayes's rule in the Anderson/Holt experiment, and 64 percent in Marc Willinger and Anthony Ziegelmeyet, *Are More Informed Agents Able to Shatter Information Cascades in the Lab*, in *The Economics of Networks: Interaction and Behaviours* 291, 304 (Patrick Cohendet et al. eds. 1996).

17 *See id.* at 291.

18 Anderson and Holt, *supra* note 14, at 859.

19 *See* Hirshleifer, *supra* note 5, at 197–98.

20 *See* Willinger and Ziegelmeyet, *supra* note 16.

21 *See id.* at 305.

22 *See* Cass R. Sunstein, *#Republic* (2016), for some ideas.

23 *See* Hung and Plott, *supra*. note 15, at 1511.

24 *See id.* at 1517.

25 *See id.* at 1515.

26 *See* John Stuart Mill, *On Liberty*, in *Utilitarianism: On Liberty; Considerations on Representative Government* (H. B. Acton ed. 1972).

27 Joseph Henrich et al., *Group Report: What Is the Role of Culture in Bounded Rationality?*, in *Bounded Rationality: The Adaptive Toolbox* 356 (Gerd Gigerenzer and Reinhard Selten eds. 2001).

28 Edward Parson, Richard Zeckhauser, and Cary Coglianese, *Collective Silence and Individual Voice: The Logic of Information Games*, in *Collective Choice: Essays in Honor of Mancur Olson* 31 (J. Heckelman and D. Coates eds. 2003).

29 *See* Timur Kuran, *Private Truths, Public Lies* (1997). *See also* Christina Bicchieri and Yoshitaka Fukui, *The Great Illusion: Ignorance, Informational Cascades, and the Persistence of Unpopular Norms*, in *Experience, Reality, and Scientific Explanation* 89, 108–14 (M. C. Galavotti and A. Pagnini eds. 1999). For an engaging discussion, *see* Malcolm Gladwell, *The Tipping Point* (1999).

30 *See* Hans Christian Anderson, *The Emperor's New Suit*, in *Shorter Tales* (Jean Hersholt trans. 1948; originally published 1837).

31 *See* Henrich et al., *supra* note 27, at 357.

32 *See* Hung and Plott, *supra* note 15, at 1515–17.

33 *Id.* at 1516.

34 *See* Parson, Zeckhauser, and Coglianese, *supra* note 28.

35 *See id.* for helpful discussion.

36 David Grann, *Stalking Dr. Steere*, New York Times, at 52 (July 17, 2001).

37 *See* Bicchieri and Fukui, *supra* note 29, at 93.

38 Andrew Higgins, *It's a Mad, Mad, Mad-Cow World*, Wall Street Journal, at A13 (March 12, 2001; internal quotation marks omitted).

39 Alexis de Tocqueville, *The Old Regime and the French Revolution* 155 (Stuart Gilbert trans. 1955).

40 *See* Russell Hardin, *The Crippled Epistemology of Extremism*, in *Political Rationality and Extremism* 3, 16 (Albert Breton et al. eds. 2002).

41 Bicchieri and Fukui, *supra* note 29, at 114.

42 *See* Kuran, *supra* note 29.

43 *See*, for example, Larry Thompson, *The Corporate Scandals: Why They Happened and Why They May Not Happen Again*, Brookings Institution (2004; recounting the history of the Corporatep-Fraud Task Force); and Sarbanes-Oxley Act of 2002, Pub. L. 107–204 (2002).

44 *Judge Puts Pledge of Allegiance Decision on Hold*, Bulletin's Frontrunner, at www.lexis.com (June 28, 2002).

45 For a good discussion, *see* Kuran, *supra* note 29.

46 *See id.*

47 *See id.*

48 Joseph Raz, *Ethics in the Public Domain* 39 (1994).

49 *See* Amartya Sen, *Poverty and Famines* (1983).

50 *See* Edwin Cameron, *AIDS Denial in South Africa*, 5 Green Bag 415, 416–19 (2002).

51 *See* F. A. Hayek, *The Use of Knowledge in Society*, 35 Am. Econ. Rev. 519 (1945).

52 For an overview, *see Heuristics and Biases: The Psychology of Intuitive Judgment* (Thomas Gilovich et al. eds. 2002).

53 *See*, for example, Roger Noll and James Krier, *Some Implications of Cognitive Psychology for Risk Regulation*, 19 J. Legal Stud. 747 (1991).

54 *See* Paul Slovic, *The Perception of Risk* 40 (2000).

55 *See* Kuran and Sunstein, *supra* note 3.

CHAPTER 3. GROUP POLARIZATION

1 *See* Roger Brown, *Social Psychology* 203–26 (2d ed. 1985). At first glance, group polarization might be seen to be in tension with the Condorcet jury theorem, which holds that when people are answering a common question with two answers, one false and one true, and when the average probability that each voter will answer correctly exceeds 50 percent, the probability of a correct answer, by a majority of the group, increases to certainty as the size of the group increases. For a good overview, *see* Paul H. Edelman, *On Legal Interpretations of the Condorcet Jury Theorem*, 31 J. Legal Stud. 327, 329–34 (2002). The importance of the theorem lies in the demonstration that groups are likely to do better than individuals, and large groups better than small ones, if majority rule is used and if each person is more likely than not to be correct. But when group polarization is involved, individuals do not make judgments on their own; they are influenced by the judgments of others. When interdependent judgments are being made, and when some people are wrong, it is not at all clear that groups will do better than individuals. For empirical evidence, *see* Norbert Kerr et al., *Bias in*

Judgment: Comparing Individuals and Groups, 103 Psychol. Rev. 687 (1996). On some of the theoretical issues, *see* David Austen-Smith and J. S. Banks, *Information Aggregation, Rationality, and the Condorcet Jury Theorem*, 90 Am. Pol. Sci. Rev. 34 (1996).

2 *See* Brown, *supra* note 1, at 204.

3 *See id.* at 224.

4 *See* Albert Breton and Silvana Dalmazzone, *Information Control, Loss of Autonomy, and the Emergence of Political Extremism* 53–55 (Albert Breton et al. eds. 2002).

5 Group polarization can occur, however, as a result of mere exposure to the views of others. *See* Robert Baron et al., *Group Process, Group Decision, Group Action* 74 (2d ed. 1999).

6 *See* David Schkade, Cass R. Sunstein, and Daniel Kahneman, *Deliberating about Dollars: The Severity Shift*, 100 Colum. L. Rev. 1139 (2001).

7 *See id.* at 1152, 1154–55.

8 *See* Cass R. Sunstein et al., *Punitive Damages: How Juries Decide* 32–33 (2002).

9 *See id.* at 36.

10 *See* Schkade et al., *supra* note 6, at 1152, showing that in the top five outrage cases, the mean shift was 11 percent higher than in any other class of cases. The effect is more dramatic still for dollars. *See id.*, where high-dollar awards shifted upward by a significant margin. This finding is closely connected to another one: extremists are most likely to shift, and likely to shift most, as a result of discussions with one another. *See* John Turner et al., *Rediscovering the Social Group* 154–59 (1987).

11 *See* Sharon Groch, *Free Spaces: Creating Oppositional Spaces in the Disability Rights Movement*, in *Oppositional Consciousness* 65, 67–72 (Jane Mansbridge and Aldon Morris eds. 2001).

12 *See* Baron et al., *Group Process*, *supra* note 5, at 77.

13 *See* R. Hightower and L. Sayeed, *The Impact of Computer-Mediated Communication Systems on Biased Group Discussion*, 11 Computers in Human Behavior 33 (1995).

14 Patricia Wallace, *The Psychology of the Internet* 82 (2000).

15 *See* Brown, *supra* note 1, at 200–45; and Sunstein, *supra* note 8.

16 *See* Brown, *supra* note 1, at 217–22.

17 *See* Caryn Christensen and Ann Abbott, *Team Medical Decision Making*, in *Decision Making in Health Care* 271 (Gretchen Chapman and Frank A. Sonnenberg eds. 2000).

18 *See* Robert Baron et al., *Social Corroboration and Opinion Extremity*, 32 J. Experimental Soc. Psychol. 537 (1996).

19 *Id.*

20 *See* Chip Heath and Richard Gonzales, *Interaction with Others Increases Decision Confidence but Not Decision Quality: Evidence against Information Collection Views of Interactive Decision Making*, 61 Organizational Behavior and Human Decision Processes 305–26 (1997).

21 *See* Brown, *supra* note 1, at 213–17.

22 *See* Baron et al., *Group Process, supra* note 5, at 74.

23 *See id.* at 77.

24 *See* Schkade et al., *supra* note 6, at 1152, 1155–56.

25 *See id.* at 1140.

26 *See id.* at 1161–62.

27 *See* Christensen and Abbott, *supra* note 17, at 269.

28 *See* Timothy Cason and Vai-Lam Mui, *A Laboratory Study of Group Polarisation in the Team Dictator Game*, 107 Econ. J. 1465 (1997).

29 *See id.*

30 *See id.* at 1468–72.

31 This is a lesson of the study of punitive damage awards, where groups with extreme medians showed the largest shifts; *see* Schkade et al., *supra* note 6, at 1152. For other evidence, *see* Turner et al., *supra* note 10, at 158.

32 *See* Maryla Zaleska, *The Stability of Extreme and Moderate Responses in Different Situations*, in *Group Decision Making* 163, 164 (H. Brandstetter, J. H. Davis, and G. Stocker-Kreichgauer eds. 1982).

33 *See* Dominic Abrams et al., *Knowing What to Think by Knowing Who You Are: Self-Categorization and the Nature of Norm Formation, Conformity, and Group Polarization*, 29 British J. Soc. Psychol. 97, 112 (1990).

34 *See* Hans Brandstatter, *Social Emotions in Discussion Groups*, in *Dynamics of Group Decisions* (Hans Brandstatter et al. eds. 1978). Turner et al., *supra* note 10, at 154–59, attempt to use this evidence as a basis for a new synthesis, one that they call "a self-categorization theory of group polarization." *Id.* at 154.

35 *See* Brandstatter, *supra* note 34. *See* Turner et al., *supra* note 10, at 154–59, for the especially interesting implication that a group of comparative extremists will show a comparatively greater shift toward extremism. *See id.* at 158.

36 *See* Turner et al., *supra* note 10, at 151.

37 *See id.*

38 *See* Russell Spears, Martin Lee, and Stephen Lee, *De-individuation and Group Polarization in Computer-Mediated Communication*, 29 Brit. J. Soc. Psych. 123–24 (1990).

39 *See* Russell Hardin, *The Crippled Epistemology of Extremism*, in *Political Rationality and Extremism* (Albert Breton et al. eds. 2002).

40 *See* James Fishkin and Robert Luskin, *Bringing Deliberation to the Democratic Dialogue*, in *The Poll with a Human Face* 3, 29–31 (Maxwell McCombs and Amy Reynolds eds. 1999).

41 *See* Alan Blinder and John Morgan, *Are Two Heads Better than One? An Experimental Analysis of Group vs. Individual Decisionmaking*, NBER Working Paper 7909 (2000).

42 *See id.* at 44–46.

43 *See* Eugene Burnstein, *Persuasion as Argument Processing*, in *Group Decision Making* (H. Brandstetter, J. H. Davis, and G. Stocker-Kreichgauer eds. 1982).

44 *See* Brown, *supra* note 1, at 225.

45 *See* Amiram Vinokur and Eugene Burnstein, *The Effects of Partially Shared Persuasive Arguments on Group-Induced Shifts*, 29 J. Personality & Soc. Psychol. 305 (1974).

46 *See id.*

47 Brown, *supra* note 1, at 226.

48 *Id.*

49 *See* Abrams et al., *supra* note 33, at 112.

CHAPTER 4. LAW AND INSTITUTIONS

1 *See* Mathew Adler, *Expressivist Theories of Law: A Skeptical Overview*, 148 U. Pa. L. Rev. 1363 (2000).

2 *See* Robert Kagan and Jerome Skolnick, *Banning Smoking: Compliance without Enforcement*, in *Smoking Policy: Law, Politics, and Culture* (Robert L. Rabin ed. 1999).

3 *See id.*

4 *Id.* at 72.

5 *See id.* at 72–73.

6 *Id.* at 78.

7 *See* Dan M. Kahan, *Gentle Nudges v. Hard Shoves: Solving the Sticky Norms Problem*, 67 U. Chi. L. Rev. 607 (2000).

8 Some of the underlying evidence is discussed in Cass R. Sunstein, *Simpler* (2013).

9 Kagan and Skolnick, *supra* note 2, at 78.

10 *See* Stephen Coleman, Minnesota Department of Revenue, *The Minnesota Income Tax Compliance Experiment State Tax Results* 1, 5–6, 18–19 (1996), at http://www.state.mn.us.

11 *See* H. Wesley Perkins, *College Student Misperceptions of Alcohol and Other Drug Norms among Peers*, in *Designing Alcohol and Other Drug Prevention Programs in Higher Education* 177–206 (U.S. Department of Education ed. 1997).

12 *See* Luther Gulick, *Administrative Reflections from World War II* 120–25 (1948).

13 *Id.* at 120.

14 *Id.* at 121.

15 *Id.* at 120–23.

16 *Id.* at 125.

17 *Id.*

18 *Id. See also* Irving Janis, *Groupthink* (2d ed. 1982), for a set of examples of errors within democracies, when relevant institutions do not encourage dissent.

19 *See* Gulick, *supra* note 12, at 125.

20 Brutus, *Essays of Brutus*, in 2 *The Complete Anti-Federalist* 369 (H. Storing ed. 1980).

21 Alexander Hamilton, *The Federalist* No. 70, at 426–37 (Clinton Rossiter ed. 1961). Compare Asch's claim: "The clash of views generates events of far-reaching importance. I am induced to take up a particular standpoint, to view my own action as another views it. . . . Now I have within me two standpoints, my own and that of the other; both are now part of my way of thinking. In this way the limitations of my individual thinking are transcended by including the thoughts of others. I am now open to more alternatives than my own unaided comprehension would make possible. Disagreements,

when their causes are intelligible, can enrich and strengthen, rather than injure, our sense of objectivity." Solomon Asch, *Social Psychology* 131–32 (1952). From a quite different discipline, John Rawls writes in similar terms: "In everyday life the exchange of opinion with others checks our partiality and widens our perspective; we are made to see things from the standpoint of others and the limits of our vision are brought home to us. . . . The benefits from discussion lie in the fact that even representative legislators are limited in knowledge and the ability to reason. No one of them knows everything the others know, or can make all the same inferences that they can draw in concert. Discussion is a way of combining information and enlarging the range of arguments." John Rawls, *A Theory of Justice* 358–59 (1971). The idea can be traced to Aristotle, suggesting that when diverse groups "all come together . . . they may surpass—collectively and as a body, although not individually—the quality of the few best. . . . When there are many who contribute to the process of deliberation, each can bring his share of goodness and moral prudence; . . . some appreciate one part, some another, and all together appreciate all." Aristotle, *Politics* 123 (E. Barker trans. 1972). Much of my discussion here has been devoted to showing why and under what circumstances this view might or might not be true.

22 Roger Sherman, 1 *Annals of Congress* 733–45 (Joseph Gale ed. 1789).

23 James Wilson, *Lectures on Law*, in 1 *The Works of James Wilson* 291 (Robert Green McCloskey ed., 1967).

24 3 *The Records of the Federal Convention of 1787*, at 359 (Max Farrand ed., rev. ed. 1966).

25 Alexander Hamilton, *The Federalist* No. 78, at 528 (J. Cooke ed. 1961).

26 James Madison, *Report of 1800*, January 7, 1800, in 17 *Papers of James Madison* 344, 346 (David Mattern et al. eds. 1991).

27 *See Miami Herald Publishing Co. v. Tornillo*, 418 US 241 (1974) (striking down a right-of-reply law).

28 *See* Anne Phillips, *The Politics of Presence* (1995); *see also* Iris Young, *Justice and the Politics of Difference* 183–91 (1994).

29 *See* Richard L. Revesz, *Environmental Regulation, Ideology, and the DC Circuit*, 83 Va. L. Rev. 1717 (1997); Frank Cross and Emerson

Tiller, *Judicial Partisanship and Obedience to Legal Doctrine*, 107 Yale L.J. 2155 (1998).

30 *See* Cass R. Sunstein et al., *Are Judges Political?* (2006); and Richard L. Revesz, *Ideology, Collegiality, and the DC Circuit*, 85 Va. L. Rev. 805, 808 (1999). *See also* the introduction, note 3, for many references. Also valuable are Jonathan P. Kastellec, *Hierarchical and Collegial Politics on the U.S. Courts of Appeals*, 73 J. Pol. 345 (2011); Jonathan P. Kastellec, *Racial Diversity and Judicial Influence on Appellate Courts*, 57 Am. J. Pol. Sci. 167 (2013); William Landes et al., *Rational Judicial Behavior: A Statistical Study*, 1 J. Legal Analysis 775 (2009).

31 *See* Revesz, *Ideology, supra* note 30, at 805, 808.

32 *See id.* at 808.

33 Calculated from Revesz, *Environmental Regulation, supra* note 29, at 1752.

34 *See id.* at 1754.

35 See Landes et al., *supra* note 30; Sunstein et al., *Are Judges Political? supra* note 30.

36 *See* Thomas Miles and Cass R. Sunstein, *The Real World of Arbitrariness Review*, 75 U. Chi. L. Rev. 761 (2008); Revesz, *Environmental Regulation, supra* note 29, at 1754.

37 *See* Miles and Sunstein, *supra* note 36.

38 *See id.*

39 *See* Revesz, *Environmental Regulation, supra* note 29, at 1754.

40 *See id.* at 1754.

41 *See id.* at 1753.

42 *See id.*

43 *See* Cross and Tiller, *supra* note 29, at 2155. Notably, panel effects and whistleblower effects are not found in a more recent, comprehensive study. See Kent H. Barnett et al., *Administrative Law's Political Dynamics*, 71 Vand. L. Rev. 1463 (2018).

44 *See Chevron v. NRDC*, 467 US 837 (1984).

45 *See* Cross and Tiller, *supra* note 29, at 2169.

46 Constructed on the basis of data in Cross and Tiller, *id.*, at 2172–73.

47 *See id.* at 2174–76. Note, however, that Barnett et al., *supra* note 43, find no whistleblower effects.

48 *See* Cross and Tiller, *supra* note 29, at 2174–76.

49 *See* Revesz, *Environmental Regulation, supra* note 29, at 1755.

50 Landes et al., *supra* note 30; Sunstein et al., *supra* note 30.

51 *See* Robert Baron et al., *Group Process, Group Decision, Group Action* 74 (2d ed. 1999).

52 *See* Revesz, *Environmental Regulation, supra* note 29, at 2175.

53 *See* David A. Strauss and Cass R. Sunstein, *The Senate, the Constitution, and the Confirmation Process*, 101 Yale L.J. 1491 (1992).

54 *See Hopwood v. Texas*, 78 F.3d 932, 944 (5th Cir. 1996); *Grutter v. Bollinger*, 288 F.3d 732 (6th Cir. 2002).

55 *See Regents of the Univ. of Cal. v. Bakke*, 438 US 265 (1978 [opinion of Powell, J.]).

56 *See id.* at 311–12.

57 *Id.* at 313.

58 *Id.*

59 *Id.* at 314.

60 *Id.*

61 *See id.* at 316–30.

62 *Id.* at 317.

63 *Id.*

64 See *Grutter v. Bollinger*, 539 US 306 (2003); and *Gratz v. Bollinger*, 539 US 244 (2003).

65 *See City of Richmond v. Croson*, 488 US 469, 477 (1989).

66 *See United States v. Paradise*, 480 US 149 (1987); and *Local No. 93, International Association of Firefighters v. Cleveland*, 478 US 616 (1987).

67 For general discussion, *see* Kathleen M. Sullivan, *Sins of Discrimination: Last Term's Affirmative Action Cases*, 100 Harv. L. Rev. 78, 96 (1986): "Public and private employers might choose to implement affirmative action for many reasons other than to purge their own past sins of discrimination. The Jackson school board, for example, said it had done so in part to improve the quality of education in Jackson—whether by improving black students' performance or by dispelling for black and white students alike any idea that white supremacy governs our social institutions. Other employers might advance different forward-looking reasons for

affirmative action: improving their services to black constituencies, averting racial tension over the allocation of jobs in a community, or increasing the diversity of a work force, to name but a few examples. Or they might adopt affirmative action simply to eliminate from their operations all de facto embodiment of a system of racial caste. All of these reasons aspire to a racially integrated future, but none reduces to 'racial balancing for its own sake.'"

68 *See* Sandra Day O'Connor, *Thurgood Marshall: The Influence of a Reconteur*, 44 Stan. L. Rev. 1217, 1217, 1220 (1992).

INDEX

ABOUT THE AUTHOR

Cass R. Sunstein is the Robert Walmsley University Professor at Harvard. From 2009 to 2012, he served as the Administrator of the White House Office of Information and Regulatory Affairs. He is the bestselling coauthor of *Nudge: Improving Decisions about Health, Wealth, and Happiness* and author of *The World According to Star Wars*.